A Quick and Tasty
100 Easy Microwave Recipes

Your Healthy Lifestyle With Beautiful Pictures

By Olivia Anderson

Copyright © by Olivia Anderson

All rights reserved. ***Easy Microwave Recipes*** eBook is licensed for your enjoyment only and may not be re-sold or given to others. If you would like to share this eBook with another person, please purchase an additional copy for each recipient. If you are reading this eBook and did not purchase it, or it was not purchased for your use only, please return it and purchase your copy. Thank you for respecting the hard work of the author.

No part of this eBook may be reproduced or transmitted in any form or by any means, electronic or mechanical, including photocopying, recording, or by any information storage and retrieval system, without written permission from the author.

The recipes in this book are to be followed as written. The publisher is not responsible for your specific health or allergy needs that may require medical supervision. The publisher is not responsible for any adverse reactions to the recipes contained in this book.

This is a work of non-fiction. Names, characters, places, brands, media, and incidents are either the product of the author's imagination or are used fictitiously. The author acknowledges the trademarked status and trademark owners of various products referenced in this non-fiction work.

Introduction

Welcome to **"A Quick and Tasty Cookbook with 100 Easy Microwave Recipes"** by Olivia Anderson, a culinary journey crafted with the modern, time-pressed food lover in mind.

Cooking takes a backseat in a world where time is at a premium, and our lifestyles are ever more fast-paced. Olivia believes it doesn't have to be this way. This book is a testament to her conviction that excellent, wholesome meals can be prepared quickly and effortlessly using a tool many of us already possess - the microwave.

In this collection, you'll find 100 carefully curated recipes designed to cater to various tastes and dietary needs while adhering to the convenience of microwave cooking. Every recipe is simple, delicious, and easy to follow, from quick breakfasts to delicious dinners, hearty soups, and decadent desserts.

Beyond recipes, Olivia shares tips and tricks to elevate your microwave cooking experience, ensuring every meal is quick and full of flavor and nutritional value. Whether you're a novice in the kitchen or a seasoned cook short on time, this book is your guide to creating great meals in minutes, all with the power of the microwave.

Embrace the ease and simplicity of microwave cooking with **"A Quick and Tasty Cookbook with 100 Easy Microwave Recipes."** Discover new favorites, reinvent meal times, and love fast, flavorful cuisine. This is not just a cookbook; it's a new way of approaching your kitchen, meals, and precious time.

Let Olivia Anderson help you make mealtime quick, tasty, and satisfying.

Table of Contents

Chapter 1: Breezy Breakfasts in Minutes 8
- 01: Scrambled Eggs With Slices of Bacon 8
- 02: Fresh Sweet Cinnamon Rolls 10
- 03: Homemade Chocolate Chip Banana Bread 12
- 04: Apple Pancake With Cinnamon Powder 14
- 05: Homemade Chorizo Breakfast Burritos 16
- 06: French Toasts With Apple Caramelized 18
- 07: Rice Cakes With Peanut Butter and Banana 20
- 08: Freshly Baked Blueberry Muffins 22
- 09: Morning Breakfast Fried Egg 24
- 10: Vanilla Mugcake With Honey 26

Chapter 2: Marvelous Mid-Morning Munchies 28
- 11: Homemade Cheesy Spinach Quiche 28
- 12: Cheddar Scones Cheese Biscuits 30
- 13: Tender Minced Lamb 32
- 14: Cream Cheese Strawberry Stuffed French Toast 34
- 15: Creamy Scrambled Eggs 36
- 16: Bagel With Smoked Salmon 38
- 17: Healthy Fruity Pancake Stack 40
- 18: Mini Croissant With Ham 42
- 19: Sunny Side Egg and Shrimp With Salsa Sandwich 44
- 20: Healthy Avocado Turkey Sandwich 46

Chapter 3: Lightning Quick & Luscious Lunches 48
- 21: Chicken Rice Soup With Vegetables 48
- 22: Greek Salad With Feta 50
- 23: Tagliatelle Pasta With Creamy 52
- 24: Delicious Sauteed Shrimp 54
- 25: Delicious Fresh Chicken Caesar Wrap 56
- 26: Smoked Bistro Turkey Panini 58

27: Speedy Prawn Stir-Fry 60

28: Salmon Teriyaki Rice Bowl 62

29: Vegetarian Quesadilla With Cheese Beans 64

30: Grilled Curry Lime Chicken Skewers 66

Chapter 4: Afternoon Delights for Instant Cravings 68

31: Cinnamon Sugar Soft Pretzels 68

32: Hummus Dip With Pita Bread 70

33: Thai Style Spicy Chicken Wings 72

34: Hot Popcorn in the Microwave 74

35: Kale Chip Covered 76

36: Italian Pizzette Mini Pizza Bites 78

37: Creamy Avocado Dip With Cilantro 80

38: S'More Dip Cookies Chocolate and Marshmallow 82

39: Bacon Stuffed Mushroom Caps 84

40: Caramelized Corn Cakes 86

Chapter 5: Dashing Dinners Done in Jiffy 88

41: Pesto Chicken Fettuccini 88

42: Whole Wheat Pasta With Vegetables 90

43: Classic Caesar Salad With Grilled Chicken Fillet 92

44: Eggplant Parmigiana 94

45: Sweet Potato Stuffed 96

46: Turkey Meatballs With Zucchini Noodles 98

47: Garlic King Prawn Wood Fired Pizza 100

48: Hearty Sausage Casserole 102

49: Grilled Salmon Steak 104

50: Fried Tofu With Sesame Seeds 106

Chapter 6: Midnight Munchies for the Night Owls 108

51: Cheesy Breadsticks 108

52: Chocolate Mug Cakes 110

53: Energy Protein Balls 112

54: Healthy Trail Mix Snack 114

55: Pepperoni Mini Pizza Bagels 116

56: Organic Apple Cinnamon Chips 118

57: Hot Chocolate With Salted Caramel 120

58: Roasted Chickpeas 122

59: Rustic Potato Skins With Cheese 124

60: Baked Orange Sweet Potato Fries 126

Chapter 7: Seafood Splendors Straight from Microwave 128

61: Fried Butter Garlic Shrimp 128

62: Chinese Seafood Medley of Shrimp 130

63: Fried Fish Fillet and Vegetables 132

64: Spicy Cajun Shrimp With Rice 134

65: Seafood Gumbo 136

66: Baja Fish Tacos With Mango Salsa 138

67: Chili Garlic Prawns Starter 140

68: New England Clam Chowder 142

69: Portobello Mushroom Stuffed With Crab 144

70: Seasoned Baked Lobster Tails 146

Chapter 8: Sippable Delights Drinks & Smoothies 148

71: Hot Mulled Apple Cider 148

72: Delicious Chocolate Stripped Croissants 150

73: Healthy Ginger Tea With Lemon 152

74: Vegan Almond & Coconut Chocolate Smoothie 154

75: Pumpkin Spice Late With Cinnamon 156

76: Milk Shakes With Blackberries 158

77: Pineapple Smoothie 160

78: Strawberry Banana Smoothie Bowl 162

79: A Hearty and Healthy Oatmeal 164

80: Tea With Milk or Chai Latte 166

Chapter 9: Super Speedy Super Fresh Salads 168

   81: Warm Autumn Quinoa Salad 168

   82: Salad With Shrimps 170

   83: Chickpea Salad With Tomatoes 172

   84: Teriyaki Chicken With Salad 174

   85: Southwest Black Bean Lime Salad 176

   86: Cobb Salad 178

   87: Pasta Salad With Grilled Vegetables 180

   88: Italian Chopped Salad 182

   89: Blueberries Cranberry Salad 184

   90: Healthy Grilled Chicken Caesar Salad 186

Chapter 10: Decadent Desserts in a Snap 188

   91: Chocolate Lava Cake Dusted 188

   92: Creamy Rice Kheer (Khir) 190

   93: Mug Cakes With Berries 192

   94: Cinnabon Cake in Mug 194

   95: Apple Crisp With Whipped Cream 196

   96: Chocolate Chip Cookies 198

   97: Variety of Chocolate Dipped Strawberries 200

   98: Peanut Butter Chocolate Cake 202

   99: Pound Cake or Angel Food Cake 204

   100: Strawberry Cobbler Made From Ripe 206

Conclusion 208

Chapter 1: Breezy Breakfasts in Minutes

01: Scrambled Eggs With Slices of Bacon

Delight in a warm, hearty breakfast with our Scrambled Eggs and Slices of Bacon. This easy, savory dish is cooked in a microwave, perfect for those on-the-go mornings or when you need a quick meal to fuel your day.

Servings: 2

Prepping Time: 5 minutes

Cook Time: 4 minutes

Difficulty: Easy

Ingredients:

- 4 eggs
- 1/4 cup of milk
- Salt and pepper to taste
- 4 slices of bacon
- 1 tbsp of butter

Step-by-Step Preparation:

1. Crack eggs into a microwave-safe bowl, and add milk, salt, and pepper. Whisk until well combined.
2. Place bacon slices on a microwave-safe plate lined with a paper towel. Microwave on high for 2-3 minutes or until crispy.
3. Add butter to the egg mixture—microwave for 1 minute. Stir and microwave again for 1-2 minutes or until eggs are fully cooked.
4. Serve scrambled eggs with crispy bacon slices. Enjoy!

Nutritional Facts: (Per serving)

- Calories: 255
- Protein: 18g
- Fat: 19g
- Carbohydrates: 2g
- Sodium: 630mg

Experience the classic combination of creamy scrambled eggs and crispy bacon with a more straightforward cooking process using your microwave. Start your day right with this protein-rich dish, ideal for breakfast but suitable for any meal.

02: Fresh Sweet Cinnamon Rolls

Enjoy the warm, delightful taste of homemade, Fresh, Sweet Cinnamon Rolls in your kitchen. This quick and easy recipe harnesses the convenience of your microwave to bring you the comforting aroma and taste of freshly baked cinnamon rolls within minutes.

> **Servings**: 4
>
> **Prepping Time**: 15 minutes
>
> **Cook Time**: 2 minutes
>
> **Difficulty**: Easy

Ingredients:

- 1 cup all-purpose flour
- 1/2 cup milk
- 2 tablespoons granulated sugar
- 1 teaspoon baking powder
- 1/4 teaspoon salt
- 2 tablespoons unsalted butter, melted
- 1/2 teaspoon cinnamon
- 1/4 cup brown sugar

➢ For the icing: 1/2 cup powdered sugar and 1-2 tablespoons milk

Step-by-Step Preparation:

1. Combine flour, milk, granulated sugar, baking powder, and salt to form a dough.
2. Roll out the dough on a floured surface into a rectangle.
3. Spread the melted butter over the dough.
4. Mix cinnamon and brown sugar and sprinkle over the butter.
5. Roll the dough tightly and slice it into 4 rolls.
6. Place the rolls in a microwave-safe dish and microwave for 2 minutes.
7. While the rolls are cooking, mix the icing ingredients.
8. Drizzle the icing over the hot rolls before serving.

Nutritional Facts: (Per serving)

- Calories: 300
- Fat: 8g
- Carbohydrates: 52g
- Protein: 5g
- Sugar: 25g

Indulge in the sweet, spicy flavors of these Fresh Sweet Cinnamon Rolls any time you please, without the hassle of waiting for the dough to rise or baking in an oven. This simple, speedy recipe is perfect for those unexpected cravings or when you need a quick, comforting dessert or breakfast treat. Enjoy the taste of home-baked goodness with ease and convenience!

03: Homemade Chocolate Chip Banana Bread

Indulge in the comforting delight of Homemade Chocolate Chip Banana Bread, a quick and straightforward microwave recipe that transforms ripe bananas and chocolate chips into an irresistible treat. Perfect for a grab-and-go breakfast or a dessert to satiate your sweet tooth, this bread will leave you craving more.

Servings: 8 slices

Prepping Time: 15 minutes

Cook Time: 5 minutes

Difficulty: Easy

Ingredients:

- 3 ripe bananas
- 1.5 cups of all-purpose flour
- 1 cup of sugar
- 1/2 cup of unsalted butter
- 2 eggs
- 1 tsp of baking soda
- 1/2 cup of chocolate chips

- ➢ 1 tsp of vanilla extract

Step-by-Step Preparation:

1. Mash bananas in a bowl and mix in melted butter.
2. Add sugar, beaten eggs, and vanilla, stirring until well combined.
3. In a separate bowl, mix flour and baking soda. Gradually add this to the banana mixture.
4. Fold in chocolate chips.
5. Pour batter into a microwave-safe loaf dish.
6. Microwave on high for about 5 minutes or until a toothpick inserted comes out clean.

Nutritional Facts: (Per serving)

- ❖ Calories: 325
- ❖ Protein: 5g
- ❖ Carbohydrates: 53g
- ❖ Fat: 12g
- ❖ Fiber: 2g
- ❖ Sugar: 30g

Indulge your senses with this Homemade Chocolate Chip Banana Bread that's effortlessly quick to prepare. The recipe's simplicity and the heart-warming blend of bananas and chocolate chips are sure to become a family favorite. Whether you're a novice baker or an experienced cook, this easy microwave bread is bound to impress.

04: Apple Pancake With Cinnamon Powder

Start your day with this delightful Apple Pancake with Cinnamon Powder recipe! Using just a microwave, you can create these fluffy and aromatic pancakes that serve as a perfect breakfast treat or snack, filled with apple goodness and the warming flavor of cinnamon.

Servings: 2

Prepping Time: 15 Minutes

Cook Time: 5 Minutes

Difficulty: Easy

Ingredients:

- 1 cup All-Purpose Flour
- 1 tsp Baking Powder
- 2 tbsp Sugar
- 1/2 tsp Cinnamon Powder
- 1/2 cup Milk
- 1 Egg
- 1 Apple, finely chopped

Step-by-Step Preparation:

1. Combine flour, baking powder, sugar, and cinnamon in a bowl.
2. In a separate bowl, whisk together milk and egg.
3. Slowly add the wet mixture to the dry ingredients until combined.
4. Fold in the chopped apple.
5. Pour 1/4 cup of batter onto a microwave-safe plate and microwave for 1-2 minutes or until the pancake rises and sets.
6. Repeat with the remaining batter. Serve warm with additional cinnamon and apple slices if desired.

Nutritional Facts: (Per serving)

- ❖ Calories: 350
- ❖ Protein: 8g
- ❖ Carbohydrates: 60g
- ❖ Fat: 8g
- ❖ Fiber: 3g
- ❖ Sugar: 20g

Indulge in the homemade simplicity of these Apple Pancakes with Cinnamon Powder. This easy microwave recipe offers a unique take on traditional pancakes, making them even more appealing. Savor the aroma of warm apples and cinnamon, enjoy the fluffy texture, and start your day with a delicious, easy-to-make breakfast.

05: Homemade Chorizo Breakfast Burritos

Experience the joy of a hearty, Mexican-inspired breakfast with this homemade Chorizo Breakfast Burritos recipe. Packed with flavorful chorizo, ripe avocado, and fresh Pico de Gallo, these burritos are an excellent start to any morning and can be quickly whipped up using a microwave.

Servings: 4

Prepping Time: 15 Minutes

Cook Time: 10 Minutes

Difficulty: Easy

Ingredients:

- 4 large tortillas
- 1 cup cooked chorizo
- 4 eggs scrambled
- 1 ripe avocado, sliced
- 1 cup Pico de Gallo
- 1 cup shredded cheese
- Salt and pepper to taste

Step-by-Step Preparation:

1. Layer each tortilla with equal portions of chorizo, scrambled eggs, avocado slices, Pico de Gallo, and shredded cheese.
2. Season with salt and pepper.
3. Roll the burritos tightly, tucking in the ends.
4. Place the burritos in the microwave and cook for about 2 minutes or until the cheese is melted.
5. Allow to cool for a minute before serving.

Nutritional Facts: (Per serving)

- Calories: 475
- Protein: 22g
- Carbs: 30g
- Fat: 30g
- Sodium: 720mg
- Fiber: 5g

Savor these Homemade Chorizo Breakfast Burritos, a perfect blend of wholesome and delicious ingredients that guarantee a satisfying meal. This easy-to-make microwave dish offers flavors that will energize your day. Enjoy this Mexican delicacy right at home!

06: French Toasts With Apple Caramelized

Indulge in the heart-warming flavors of French Toast with Apple Caramelized and Cinnamon. This easy microwave recipe pairs the comforting aroma of cinnamon with the rich sweetness of caramelized apples to create a breakfast dish that's sure to delight.

Servings: 4

Prepping Time: 10 Minutes

Cook Time: 10 Minutes

Difficulty: Easy

Ingredients:

- 8 slices of bread
- 4 eggs
- 1 cup of milk
- 1 teaspoon vanilla extract
- 2 apples, peeled and sliced
- 3 tablespoons of sugar
- 1 teaspoon cinnamon
- 1 tablespoon butter

Step-by-Step Preparation:

1. In a bowl, beat eggs, milk, and vanilla extract together. Soak each slice of bread in the mixture.
2. Place the soaked bread slices on a microwave-safe plate and microwave for 2 minutes.
3. In another bowl, mix the apples, sugar, and cinnamon. Microwave for 3-4 minutes until the apples are softened and caramelized.
4. Melt the butter in the microwave and pour over the toasted bread.
5. Top each toast with the caramelized apples and serve hot.

Nutritional Facts: (Per serving)

- Calories: 350
- Protein: 12g
- Carbohydrates: 52g
- Fat: 12g
- Saturated Fat: 5g
- Cholesterol: 170mg
- Sodium: 320mg
- Fiber: 4g
- Sugar: 28g

Enjoy this French Toast with Apple Caramelized and Cinnamon as a breakfast treat, a snack, or a dessert. Not only is this recipe incredibly easy to make, but it also packs a delicious punch with every bite. Now, who said gourmet breakfasts can't be made in a microwave?

07: Rice Cakes With Peanut Butter and Banana

Delight your palate with these easy-to-make Rice Cakes with Peanut Butter and Slices of Banana. They are perfect for a quick, healthy snack, balancing sweet and savory flavors while providing nutritious energy for the day.

Servings: 2

Prepping Time: 5 minutes

Cook Time: 2 minutes

Difficulty: Easy

Ingredients:

- 4 rice cakes
- 4 tablespoons peanut butter
- 1 ripe banana, sliced

Step-by-Step Preparation:

1. Spread a tablespoon of peanut butter evenly on each rice cake.
2. Arrange the banana slices on top of the peanut butter.
3. Microwave each prepared rice cake for 30 seconds or until warm.
4. Serve immediately.

Nutritional Facts: (Per serving)

- Calories: 215
- Protein: 6g
- Carbs: 26g
- Fat: 11g
- Fiber: 3g

Enjoy these Rice Cakes with Peanut Butter and Slices of Banana as a wholesome breakfast or a fulfilling snack. This dish is not just an energy booster but also a creative way to satisfy your sweet tooth without compromising on health. Perfect for anyone who loves to combine simplicity with great taste!

08: Freshly Baked Blueberry Muffins

Savor the sweet aroma and succulent taste of freshly baked blueberry muffins with an oat crumble topping. These muffins are a breeze to prepare, yet so delicious that they'll make you feel like a gourmet baker.

Servings: 6 Muffins

Prepping Time: 15 Minutes

Cook Time: 2 Minutes per muffin

Difficulty: Easy

Ingredients:

- 1 cup of flour
- 1/2 cup of sugar
- 1/2 cup of blueberries
- 1/2 cup of oats
- 1/4 cup of butter
- 1 egg
- 2 tsp of baking powder
- Pinch of salt

Step-by-Step Preparation:

1. Mix flour, sugar, baking powder, and salt.
2. Stir in egg until the mixture is crumbly.
3. Fold in the blueberries.
4. Fill microwave-safe muffin cups halfway with the mixture.
5. Combine oats and butter to make the crumble topping, then sprinkle on each muffin.
6. Microwave each muffin for 2 minutes or until a toothpick comes out clean.

Nutritional Facts: (Per serving)

- Calories: 240
- Protein: 4g
- Fat: 8g
- Carbohydrates: 38g
- Fiber: 2g
- Sugar: 18g

Conclude your busy day with a treat for your senses as you enjoy the tantalizing flavors of freshly baked blueberry muffins straight from the microwave. With an oat crumble topping, these muffins are a quick, easy, and delightful solution to your sweet cravings.

09: Morning Breakfast Fried Egg

Kickstart your morning with a nutritious, flavor-packed breakfast that is easy and quick to make. This microwave-friendly dish incorporates fresh vegetables, savory ham, and perfectly fried eggs for a deliciously balanced start to your day.

Servings: 1

Prepping Time: 10 minutes

Cook Time: 2 minutes

Difficulty: Easy

Ingredients:

- 1 egg
- 2 slices of ham
- 1/4 cup chopped bell peppers
- 1/4 cup chopped tomatoes
- Salt and pepper to taste
- 1 tablespoon olive oil

Step-by-Step Preparation:

1. Chop the bell peppers and tomatoes.
2. Place the ham in a microwave-safe dish, and layer the vegetables.
3. Crack the egg over the vegetables.
4. Drizzle with olive oil and season with salt and pepper.
5. Microwave on high for about 2 minutes or until the egg is cooked to your liking.

Nutritional Facts: (Per serving)

- Calories: 200
- Protein: 14g
- Fat: 14g
- Carbs: 6g
- Fiber: 2g

Delight in a breakfast that is quick to prepare but also satisfying and nutritious. The Morning Breakfast Fried Egg With Ham and Vegetables will have you facing the day with energy, thanks to its balance of protein, healthy fats, and vegetables. It's the perfect breakfast solution for busy mornings.

10: Vanilla Mugcake With Honey

Delight in a cozy, single-serve dessert with this easy Vanilla Mugcake with Honey recipe. This microwave-friendly dish is perfect for those sudden sweet cravings or when you need a quick dessert fix.

Servings: 1

Prepping Time: 5 minutes

Cook Time: 2 minutes

Difficulty: Easy

Ingredients:

- 4 tablespoons all-purpose flour
- 2 tablespoons sugar
- 1/8 teaspoon baking powder
- a pinch of salt
- 3 tablespoons milk
- 2 tablespoons vegetable oil
- 1/4 teaspoon pure vanilla extract
- 1 tablespoon honey

Step-by-Step Preparation:

1. Combine flour, sugar, baking powder, and salt in a microwave-safe mug.
2. Stir in the milk, oil, and vanilla extract until smooth.
3. Microwave on high for about 90 seconds or until the cake has risen and set.
4. Let cool for a minute, then drizzle honey on top. Enjoy while warm!

Nutritional Facts: (Per serving)

- Calories: 410 kcal
- Carbohydrates: 50g
- Protein: 4g
- Fat: 22g
- Saturated Fat: 18g
- Cholesterol: 3mg
- Sodium: 30mg
- Potassium: 68mg
- Sugar: 27g

Indulge in the simple pleasure of homemade dessert anytime with this Vanilla Mugcake with Honey. Not only does it satiate your sweet tooth, but it's also a fun, speedy kitchen project that requires minimal ingredients and effort. Treat yourself to this little mug of joy!

Chapter 2: Marvelous Mid-Morning Munchies

11: Homemade Cheesy Spinach Quiche

Dive into a healthy, delicious start to your day with this Homemade Cheesy Spinach Quiche. This microwave-friendly dish infuses the creamy cheese flavors with nutritious spinach in a simple and quick recipe, perfect for a laid-back weekend brunch.

Servings: 4

Prepping Time: 10 Minutes

Cook Time: 20 Minutes

Difficulty: Easy

Ingredients:

- 4 Large Eggs
- 2 Cups Fresh Spinach
- 1 Cup Shredded Cheddar Cheese
- 1/2 Cup Milk

- 1/2 Onion, chopped
- Salt and Pepper to taste

Step-by-Step Preparation:

1. Whisk eggs, milk, salt, and Pepper in a bowl.
2. Stir in the chopped spinach, Onion, and cheese.
3. Pour the mixture into a microwave-safe dish.
4. Cook in the microwave for 5 minutes, stir, and then microwave for another 10-15 minutes until set.
5. Let it cool for a few minutes before serving.

Nutritional Facts: (Per serving)

- Calories: 210
- Protein: 14g
- Carbohydrates: 5g
- Fats: 15g
- Fiber: 1g
- Sugars: 3g

Rejoice in the seamless fusion of nutritious greens and delectable cheese with this Homemade Cheesy Spinach Quiche. With minimal preparation time and a straightforward cooking method, it's a delicious and wholesome option for your leisurely brunches or quick weekday breakfasts. Enjoy this delightfully easy, microwaveable treat, adding a savory kick to your mornings.

12: Cheddar Scones Cheese Biscuits

Indulge in the simplicity and savory delight of Cheddar Scones, a perfect blend of light, fluffy texture, and sharp cheese taste. This classic British dish finds a modern twist in your kitchen.

Servings: 4

Prepping Time: 15 minutes

Cook Time: 2 minutes per scone

Difficulty: Easy

Ingredients:

- 2 cups self-raising flour
- 1/2 cup unsalted butter
- 1 cup grated cheddar cheese
- 3/4 cup milk
- Pinch of salt

Step-by-Step Preparation:

1. Mix flour and butter until crumbly.
2. Stir in cheese, then add milk to form a dough.

3. Split dough into 4 and shape into scones.
4. Microwave each scone for 2 minutes or until they rise and turn golden.

Nutritional Facts: (Per serving)

- ❖ Calories: 455
- ❖ Fat: 25g
- ❖ Carbs: 45g
- ❖ Protein: 12g

Revel in the satisfaction of creating homemade Cheddar Scones, offering a mouth-watering blend of melt-in-your-mouth goodness and warm, hearty comfort. Whether it's for a quick breakfast, afternoon tea, or a delightful side to your soup, these cheese biscuits are a versatile treat for any occasion.

13: Tender Minced Lamb

Indulge in a deliciously comforting meal with this Tender Minced Lamb With Hearty Gravy Beneath Butter Mash recipe. It's a satisfying combination of succulent lamb and rich gravy, topped with buttery mashed potatoes, all cooked conveniently in your microwave.

Servings: 4

Prepping Time: 20 minutes

Cook Time: 30 minutes

Difficulty: Easy

Ingredients:

- 500g minced lamb
- 1 large onion, chopped
- 2 cloves garlic, minced
- 1 cup beef broth
- 1 cup red wine
- 2 tablespoons flour
- 2 cups mashed potatoes
- 2 tablespoons butter

> Salt and pepper to taste

Step-by-Step Preparation:

1. Mix the lamb, onion, and garlic in a microwave-safe dish, then cook on high for 5 minutes.
2. Stir in the flour, followed by the broth and wine.
3. Cook for another 15 minutes, stirring halfway through.
4. Mix the mashed potatoes with butter in a separate dish and microwave until hot.
5. Layer the lamb mixture with the buttered mash, then microwave for 5 minutes.
6. Season with salt and pepper before serving.

Nutritional Facts: (Per serving)

- Calories: 450
- Proteins: 28g
- Carbs: 26g
- Fat: 24g

Unwind with a comforting dish that is as delicious and easy to make. This Tender Minced Lamb With Hearty Gravy Beneath Butter Mash brings gourmet tastes to your microwave, promising a delectable meal without the hassle of extensive kitchen work. Enjoy this delightful combination of flavors any day of the week.

14: Cream Cheese Strawberry Stuffed French Toast

Savor the sweet indulgence of a classic French breakfast with a nutritious twist in our Healthy Cream Cheese Strawberry Stuffed French Toast. This dish combines strawberries' fresh, bright flavors and rich, creamy cheese texture in a light yet satisfying way using your microwave.

Servings: 2

Prepping Time: 10 minutes

Cook Time: 3 minutes

Difficulty: Easy

Ingredients:

- 4 slices of whole-grain bread
- 1/2 cup of strawberries, chopped
- 1/2 cup of low-fat cream cheese
- 2 eggs
- 1/2 cup of almond milk
- 1 teaspoon of vanilla extract
- 1 tablespoon of honey

Step-by-Step Preparation:

1. Spread cream cheese on two slices of bread and add chopped strawberries.
2. Cover with remaining bread slices to form sandwiches.
3. Whisk together eggs, almond milk, vanilla extract, and honey in a bowl.
4. Dip the sandwiches into the egg mixture, ensuring they're fully coated.
5. Place on a microwave-safe dish and microwave on high for 3 minutes, flipping halfway through.

Nutritional Facts: (Per serving)

- Calories: 350
- Protein: 15g
- Carbs: 40g
- Fat: 15g
- Fiber: 6g
- Sugar: 12g

Enjoy the delightful balance of luscious cream cheese, juicy strawberries, and fluffy French toast without guilt. This easy microwave recipe is perfect for those busy mornings when you need a quick yet satisfying breakfast or to pamper yourself with a healthy and delicious treat.

15: Creamy Scrambled Eggs

Indulge in the morning delight of Soft, Creamy Scrambled Eggs cooked in a cast iron skillet, accompanied by sweet cherry tomatoes. A perfect balance of simplicity and luxury, this microwave recipe promises a memorable start to your day with its superb taste and texture.

Servings: 2

Prepping Time: 5 Minutes

Cook Time: 2 Minutes

Difficulty: Easy

Ingredients:

- 4 Large Eggs
- 1/4 Cup of Full Fat Milk
- Salt and Pepper to taste
- 1 Tablespoon of Unsalted Butter
- 1/2 Cup of Cherry Tomatoes

Step-by-Step Preparation:

1. Crack the eggs into a bowl, and add milk, salt, and Pepper. Whisk until blended.
2. Place the butter in the cast iron skillet and microwave for 30 seconds until melted.
3. Pour the egg mixture into the skillet and microwave for 1 minute. Stir and microwave for another 30 seconds.
4. Serve the scrambled eggs with fresh cherry tomatoes on the side.

Nutritional Facts: (Per serving)

- ❖ Calories: 220 kcal
- ❖ Protein: 12 g
- ❖ Carbs: 4 g
- ❖ Fat: 17 g
- ❖ Fiber: 1 g
- ❖ Sugar: 3 g

Revamp your breakfast routine with these Soft, Creamy Scrambled Eggs and Cherry Tomatoes. This hearty microwave meal is ready in under 10 minutes, offering a combination of creamy eggs and juicy tomatoes that will leave you wanting more. It's a perfect dish for quick breakfasts, brimming with nourishment and flavor.

16: Bagel With Smoked Salmon

Start your day with a heart-healthy, delicious Everything Bagel topped with Smoked Salmon, Spinach, Red Onions, Avocado, and Cream Cheese. This easy-to-make microwave dish ensures a wholesome breakfast in no time.

Servings: 2

Prepping Time: 10 minutes

Cook Time: 1 minute

Difficulty: Easy

Ingredients:

- 2 Everything Bagels
- 4 ounces of Smoked Salmon
- 1/2 cup Spinach leaves
- 1/4 Red Onion, thinly sliced
- 1 ripe Avocado
- 4 tablespoons Cream Cheese

Step-by-Step Preparation:

1. Slice bagels in half and toast them slightly if preferred.

2. Spread cream cheese on each bagel half.
3. Lay smoked salmon, spinach, and red onions evenly on the bagel halves.
4. Cut avocado into slices and place on top of the other ingredients.
5. Microwave each prepared Bagel for 30 seconds.
6. Enjoy your healthy and hearty Bagel.

Nutritional Facts: (Per serving)

- Calories: 450
- Protein: 22g
- Carbohydrates: 45g
- Fiber: 9g
- Fat: 20g
- Sugar: 6g

Savor the richness of smoked salmon, the creaminess of the avocado, and the tanginess of cream cheese in each bite of this hearty, everything bagel. This quick and easy microwave recipe ensures a nutritious and delicious breakfast is just a few minutes away.

17: Healthy Fruity Pancake Stack

Start your day with our Healthy Fruity Pancake Stack! This easy microwave recipe features fluffy pancakes layered with delicious fruits. It's healthy, satisfying, and super easy to prepare, making breakfast fun and enjoyable.

> Servings: 2
>
> Prepping Time: 10 minutes
>
> Cook Time: 5 minutes
>
> Difficulty: Easy

Ingredients:

- 1 cup whole wheat pancake mix
- 3/4 cup water
- 1/2 cup mixed berries
- 1 banana, sliced
- 1 tablespoon honey
- Greek yogurt for topping

Step-by-Step Preparation:

1. In a bowl, mix the pancake mix with water until smooth.

2. Pour 1/4 cup of the batter into a microwave-safe dish and cook for 1 minute in the microwave.
3. Repeat until all batter is used.
4. Stack the pancakes, alternating with layers of mixed berries and sliced bananas.
5. Drizzle with honey and top with Greek yogurt.

Nutritional Facts: (Per serving)

- Calories: 280
- Protein: 6g
- Carbohydrates: 50g
- Fat: 5g
- Fiber: 7g

Start your day with a breakfast that tastes like a treat, yet it's still healthy! Enjoy these Healthy Fruity Pancake Stacks straight from your microwave and bring a touch of creativity to your morning routine. Perfect for health-conscious yet still enjoying a flavorful and satisfying breakfast.

18: Mini Croissant With Ham

Enjoy the savory elegance of these Mini Croissants with Ham, Cheese, and Red Onion Canapés. Easy to make, these gourmet delights are perfect for brunch, dinner parties, or even just a quiet night in. They are as delicious as they are beautiful, sure to wow any guest.

Servings: 6

Prepping Time: 10 minutes

Cook Time: 2 minutes

Difficulty: Easy

Ingredients:

- 12 Mini Croissants
- 12 thin slices of Ham
- 1 Red Onion, thinly sliced
- 100g Cheese, thinly sliced
- 1 tablespoon of Olive oil

Step-by-Step Preparation:

1. Split the mini croissants in half.

2. Place a slice of ham, red onion, and cheese on the bottom half of each croissant.
3. Drizzle a bit of olive oil over the toppings.
4. Cover with the top half of the croissant.
5. Arrange them on a microwave-safe dish.
6. Microwave for 2 minutes or until the cheese melts.
7. Serve immediately while warm.

Nutritional Facts: (Per serving)

- Calories: 150
- Proteins: 6g
- Carbs: 15g
- Fat: 7g
- Fiber: 1g

Sink your teeth into these luscious Mini Croissant Canapés. A soft buttery croissant envelopes the perfect balance of creamy cheese, salty ham, and crunchy onion. With such an effortless recipe, you can serve up gourmet canapés at home anytime, making every day feel like a special occasion.

19: Sunny Side Egg and Shrimp With Salsa Sandwich

Indulge in a flavorful culinary journey with our Homemade Sunny Side Up Egg and Shrimp with Salsa Sauce Open Sandwich. It's a delicious and easy microwave recipe, perfect for quick breakfasts or brunches, that offers an explosion of taste and texture in each bite.

Servings: 2

Prepping Time: 10 minutes

Cook Time: 5 minutes

Difficulty: Easy

Ingredients:

- 2 slices of bread
- 2 eggs
- 4 large shrimps, peeled and deveined
- 1 cup salsa sauce
- 2 tbsp olive oil
- Salt and pepper to taste

Step-by-Step Preparation:

1. Heat olive oil in a microwave-safe dish and add shrimp. Microwave for 1-2 minutes or until they turn pink.
2. In the same dish, crack open the eggs carefully, ensuring the yolks remain intact. Microwave for another 1-2 minutes or until the whites are set.
3. Spread salsa sauce on each bread slice.
4. Carefully place the microwaved sunny-side-up egg and shrimp on the bread.
5. Season with salt and pepper. Your open sandwich is ready to serve.

Nutritional Facts: (Per serving)

- ❖ Calories: 350
- ❖ Fat: 16g
- ❖ Carbohydrates: 28g
- ❖ Protein: 20g
- ❖ Sodium: 520mg
- ❖ Fiber: 3g

This homemade sunny-side-up egg and shrimp with salsa sauce open sandwich provides a delicious spin to your regular breakfast routine. It's quick, easy, and packed with flavors. Pair it with hot coffee or tea for a wholesome start to your day. Enjoy this easy-to-prepare, microwave-friendly dish that's sure to impress!

20: Healthy Avocado Turkey Sandwich

Indulge in the exquisite taste of a Healthy Avocado Turkey Sandwich with Swiss Cheese and Bacon. This easy-to-prepare dish marries nutrition with delightful flavors, perfect for a quick lunch or hearty snack.

Servings: 2

Prepping Time: 10 Minutes

Cook Time: 1 Minute

Difficulty: Easy

Ingredients:

- 4 slices of whole-grain bread
- 4 pieces of turkey breast
- 2 pieces of Swiss cheese
- 2 strips of cooked bacon
- 1 ripe avocado, sliced
- Salt and pepper to taste

Step-by-Step Preparation:

1. Lay out the slices of bread and place a piece of turkey on each.

2. Top with Swiss cheese and bacon.
3. Add sliced avocado and sprinkle with salt and pepper.
4. Microwave each sandwich for 1 minute or until the cheese is melted.
5. Serve immediately.

Nutritional Facts: (Per serving)

- Calories: 435
- Fat: 20g
- Protein: 30g
- Carbs: 40g
- Fiber: 10g

Relish this delicious and hearty Healthy Avocado Turkey Sandwich with Swiss Cheese and Bacon. It's the ideal blend of health and flavor, packed with protein, healthy fats, and fiber. This easy microwave recipe will satisfy you whether for a quick weekday lunch or a casual weekend brunch.

Chapter 3: Lightning Quick & Luscious Lunches

21: Chicken Rice Soup With Vegetables

Unleash the comforting charm of a classic home-cooked meal with our easy microwave Chicken Rice Soup recipe. Packed with nutritious vegetables, tender chicken, and deliciously cooked rice, it's a flavorful symphony perfect for a cozy evening at home.

> **Servings:** 4
>
> **Prepping Time:** 15 Minutes
>
> **Cook Time:** 25 Minutes
>
> **Difficulty:** Easy

Ingredients:

> - 2 cups of diced chicken breast
> - 1 cup of cooked rice
> - 1 diced onion
> - 2 minced garlic cloves

- ➤ 1 cup of diced carrots
- ➤ 1 cup of diced celery
- ➤ 4 cups of chicken broth
- ➤ Salt and pepper to taste
- ➤ Fresh parsley for garnish
- ➤ 4 slices of bread

Step-by-Step Preparation:

1. Combine chicken, onion, garlic, carrots, and celery in a microwave-safe bowl.
2. Cover the bowl and microwave for 5 minutes or until the chicken is cooked.
3. Stir in the cooked rice and chicken broth. Season with salt and pepper.
4. Cover the bowl and microwave for another 20 minutes.
5. Stir the soup, garnish with fresh parsley, and serve with a slice of bread.

Nutritional Facts: (Per serving)

- ❖ Calories: 340 kcal
- ❖ Protein: 24g
- ❖ Carbohydrates: 35g
- ❖ Dietary Fiber: 4g
- ❖ Sugars: 4g
- ❖ Fat: 10g
- ❖ Saturated Fat: 2g
- ❖ Sodium: 900mg

Savor the delight of a traditional chicken rice soup with a twist of convenience in your kitchen. This simple, microwave-friendly recipe delivers a heartwarming meal loaded with the goodness of chicken and vegetables, perfect for a quick lunch or dinner. Keep a loaf of bread handy to soak up every last delicious drop!

22: Greek Salad With Feta

Embrace the vibrant, fresh flavors of the Mediterranean with this easy Greek Salad with Feta recipe. It is made in the microwave and combines crunchy vegetables, tangy feta cheese, and a simple dressing to create a refreshing and delicious dish.

Servings: 4

Prepping Time: 10 minutes

Cook Time: 2 minutes

Difficulty: Easy

Ingredients:

- 2 large cucumbers, diced
- 4 ripe tomatoes, diced
- 1 red onion, thinly sliced
- 1 cup Kalamata olives
- 200g Feta cheese, crumbled
- 1/4 cup olive oil
- Juice of 1 lemon
- 1 tablespoon dried oregano

> Salt and pepper to taste

Step-by-Step Preparation:

1. Combine cucumbers, tomatoes, red onion, and olives in a microwave-safe dish.
2. Microwave on high for 1 minute.
3. Mix the olive oil, lemon juice, oregano, salt, and pepper in a separate bowl.
4. Drizzle the dressing over the warmed vegetables and add the crumbled feta.
5. Microwave for another 1 minute.
6. Toss gently to combine before serving.

Nutritional Facts: (Per serving)

- Calories: 265
- Protein: 8g
- Carbohydrates: 15g
- Fat: 20g
- Sodium: 740mg
- Fiber: 4g

The Greek Salad with Feta perfectly embodies healthy eating that doesn't compromise on flavor. Quick to prepare in a microwave, this salad brings a taste of the Mediterranean to your table. Enjoy it as a light lunch or an impressive side dish at dinner. Enjoy the balance of tang, crunch, and freshness in every bite!

23: Tagliatelle Pasta With Creamy

Enjoy Italian cuisine by indulging in this delightfully creamy tagliatelle pasta with wild garlic sauce. It's easy to make, bursting with flavors, and cooked perfectly in a microwave, making it a perfect choice for a quick, comforting meal.

Servings: 4

Prepping Time: 15 minutes

Cook Time: 10 minutes

Difficulty: Easy

Ingredients:

- 400g tagliatelle pasta
- 1 cup wild garlic leaves, chopped
- 1 cup heavy cream
- 1/2 cup Parmesan cheese, grated
- Salt and pepper to taste

Step-by-Step Preparation:

1. Cook the pasta in the microwave as per the package instructions.

2. Combine the chopped garlic leaves, heavy cream, and Parmesan cheese in a microwave-safe bowl.
3. Cook this mixture in the microwave for 2-3 minutes until hot and creamy.
4. Drain the pasta, mix it with the sauce, season with salt and pepper.
5. Serve immediately, garnished with a sprinkle of Parmesan cheese.

Nutritional Facts: (Per serving)

- Calories: 560 kcal
- Protein: 18g
- Carbohydrates: 64g
- Fat: 25g
- Saturated Fat: 14g
- Sodium: 440mg
- Fiber: 3g
- Sugar: 3g

Indulge your taste buds with this sumptuous Tagliatelle Pasta with a Creamy Wild Garlic Sauce, bringing a piece of Italian cuisine to your table. It's perfect for a quick weekday dinner, a date night, or to impress your guests. This pasta dish guarantees a symphony of flavors in every bite!

24: Delicious Sauteed Shrimp

Welcome to a speedy culinary journey through Louisiana's deep south with an effortless microwave twist. This delicious Sauteed Shrimp with Cajun Seasoning and Lime recipe combines succulent shrimp with the tangy pop of lime and the bold heat of Cajun spice. It's a meal that brings the magic of New Orleans straight to your kitchen.

Servings: 4

Prepping Time: 10 Minutes

Cook Time: 5 Minutes

Difficulty: Easy

Ingredients:

- 1 lb of peeled and deveined shrimp
- 2 tablespoons of Cajun seasoning
- 1 tablespoon of olive oil
- Zest and juice of one lime
- Salt to taste
- Chopped parsley for garnish

Step-by-Step Preparation:

1. Mix shrimp, Cajun seasoning, olive oil, zest, lime juice, and salt in a microwave-safe bowl.
2. Microwave high for 3-5 minutes or until the shrimp are pink and cooked. Stir halfway through.
3. Garnish with chopped parsley and serve immediately.

Nutritional Facts: (Per serving)

- Calories: 120
- Protein: 23g
- Carbohydrates: 1g
- Fat: 2g
- Sodium: 260mg

With this quick and easy dish, you don't have to be a master chef to enjoy the sizzling flavors of the Bayou. Delicious Sauteed Shrimp with Cajun Seasoning and Lime is more than just a meal—it's an irresistible taste journey you can whip up in minutes from the comfort of your microwave.

25: Delicious Fresh Chicken Caesar Wrap

Step into the quick and easy cuisine world with this Delicious Homemade Fresh Chicken Caesar Wrap recipe. An ideal meal for busy individuals, this microwaveable dish blends savory chicken, crisp lettuce, and creamy Caesar dressing, all nestled within a soft tortilla wrap.

> Servings: 4
>
> Prepping Time: 10 minutes
>
> Cook Time: 2 minutes
>
> Difficulty: Easy

Ingredients:

- 2 cooked chicken breasts, sliced
- 4 large tortilla wraps
- 2 cups of Romaine lettuce, chopped
- 1 cup of Caesar dressing
- 1/2 cup of Parmesan cheese, shredded
- 1/2 cup of croutons
- Salt and pepper to taste

Step-by-Step Preparation:

1. Evenly distribute chicken, lettuce, Caesar dressing, Parmesan cheese, and croutons onto each tortilla.
2. Sprinkle with salt and pepper according to taste.
3. Roll up the wraps, ensuring that all ingredients are enclosed.
4. Microwave each wrap for 30 seconds or until warm.

Nutritional Facts: (Per serving)

- Calories: 450
- Protein: 30g
- Carbohydrates: 30g
- Fat: 22g
- Sodium: 800mg
- Fiber: 3g

Relish the flavorful journey with every bite of this Delicious Homemade Fresh Chicken Caesar Wrap. Ideal for a quick lunch or a leisurely dinner, this recipe proves that you don't need hours in the kitchen to prepare an appealing and satisfying meal. Happy microwaving!

26: Smoked Bistro Turkey Panini

Enjoy the warmth of a café right at home with our easy and quick Smoked Bistro Turkey Panini. Packed with provolone cheese, homemade pesto, and fresh tomatoes, this is a delightful way to elevate your lunch or dinner routine.

Servings: 2

Prepping Time: 10 minutes

Cook Time: 2 minutes

Difficulty: Easy

Ingredients:

- 4 slices of sourdough bread
- 6 pieces of smoked turkey
- 4 slices of provolone cheese
- 2 tablespoons of homemade pesto
- 1 tomato, sliced

Step-by-Step Preparation:

1. Spread 1 tablespoon of pesto on two slices of bread.

2. Layer 3 slices of turkey, 2 slices of provolone cheese, and tomato slices evenly over the pesto.
3. Top with the remaining bread slices.
4. Microwave each sandwich for 1 minute or until the cheese is melted.
5. Slice the panini in half and serve immediately.

Nutritional Facts: (Per serving)

- Calories: 380
- Protein: 22g
- Carbohydrates: 42g
- Fat: 15g
- Sodium: 990mg

Our Smoked Bistro Turkey Panini brings the restaurant to your kitchen in just a few minutes. It's a perfect meal when you crave something flavorful yet uncomplicated. Enjoy a side of potato chips or a fresh garden salad for a satisfying lunch.

27: Speedy Prawn Stir-Fry

Take a culinary trip to the tropics with this Speedy Prawn Stir-Fry with Zesty Spicy Flavours. Quick, simple, and delightfully spicy, this dish is perfect for a midweek dinner or casual entertaining. It combines succulent prawns with fresh herbs and spices with bold and vibrant flavors.

Servings: 4

Prepping Time: 10 minutes

Cook Time: 15 minutes

Difficulty: Easy

Ingredients:

- 400g prawns, peeled and deveined
- 2 cloves garlic, minced
- 1 red chili, sliced
- 1 bell pepper, sliced
- 200g snap peas
- 2 tablespoons soy sauce
- 1 tablespoon fish sauce
- 1 lime, juice, and zest

- ➤ Fresh cilantro for garnish
- ➤ 1 tablespoon vegetable oil

Step-by-Step Preparation:

1. Heat the vegetable oil in a large microwave-safe bowl. Add garlic, chili, bell pepper, and microwave on high for 2 minutes.
2. Stir in prawns, snap peas, soy sauce, fish sauce, lime juice, and zest. Microwave for another 3 minutes or until prawns are cooked through.
3. Garnish with fresh cilantro and serve immediately.

Nutritional Facts: (Per serving)

- ❖ Calories: 200
- ❖ Protein: 25g
- ❖ Carbohydrates: 10g
- ❖ Fat: 7g
- ❖ Fiber: 3g
- ❖ Sodium: 920mg

Set sail on a journey of delightful gastronomy with this Speedy Prawn Stir-Fry. It's easy to prepare yet always impresses with its zesty and spicy flavors. From the warmth of your microwave to the heart of your dining table, this dish will appear regularly on your weeknight menu.

28: Salmon Teriyaki Rice Bowl

This quick and nutritious Salmon Teriyaki Rice Bowl, brimming with avocado and spinach, is ideal for busy days. Made in the microwave, it offers an easy way to enjoy a hearty, balanced dish in just a few steps.

Servings: 2

Prepping Time: 10 Minutes

Cook Time: 10 Minutes

Difficulty: Easy

Ingredients:

- 2 boneless salmon fillets
- 1/4 cup teriyaki sauce
- 1 cup cooked brown rice
- 2 cups fresh spinach
- 1 ripe avocado, sliced
- 1 tablespoon sesame seeds

Step-by-Step Preparation:

1. Place the salmon fillets in a microwave-safe dish, pour over the teriyaki sauce, and microwave on high for 4-5 minutes.
2. Divide the cooked rice between two bowls.
3. Top each bowl with a portion of microwaved salmon.
4. Add spinach and sliced avocado around the salmon.
5. Drizzle any remaining teriyaki sauce over the top and sprinkle with sesame seeds.

Nutritional Facts: (Per serving)

- ❖ Calories: 540
- ❖ Protein: 35g
- ❖ Fat: 25g
- ❖ Carbohydrates: 45g
- ❖ Fiber: 8g
- ❖ Sodium: 1,200mg

Enjoy the simplicity and freshness of this Salmon Teriyaki Rice Bowl. It's not just a meal but a healthy lifestyle choice that takes minimal effort and time. Savor the delightful blend of flavors and bask in the convenience of microwave cooking.

29: Vegetarian Quesadilla With Cheese Beans

Indulge in the heart-warming flavors of Mexican cuisine right from your home kitchen with this easy-to-make Vegetarian Quesadilla. It is the perfect snack for any hunger and is filled with cheese, beans, and vegetables.

Servings: 4

Prepping Time: 15 minutes

Cook Time: 5 minutes

Difficulty: Easy

Ingredients:

- 8 Flour Tortillas
- 2 cups Shredded Cheddar Cheese
- 1 cup Cooked Black Beans
- 1 Red Bell Pepper, diced
- 1 cup Sweet Corn
- 1 Onion, diced
- 2 cloves Garlic, minced
- Salt to taste
- 1 tablespoon Olive oil

Step-by-Step Preparation:

1. Mix beans, red pepper, sweet corn, onion, Garlic, and salt in a bowl.
2. Place a tortilla on a microwave-safe plate, evenly spread the mixture, top it with cheese, then cover with another tortilla.
3. Microwave for 1 minute or until the cheese melts.
4. Let it cool for a minute before cutting it into wedges. Repeat with the remaining ingredients.
5. Serve hot with your favorite dip.

Nutritional Facts: (Per serving)

- Calories: 450 kcal
- Protein: 18g
- Fat: 20g
- Carbohydrates: 50g
- Fiber: 8g

Delve into the delectable layers of these Vegetarian Quesadillas, a snack that's not just mouth-watering but also nutritious. Enjoy this effortless microwave recipe at your next movie night or family get-together. Your culinary expertise will surely win everyone's hearts.

30: Grilled Curry Lime Chicken Skewers

Indulge in the tangy and spicy flavors of our Grilled Curry Lime Chicken Skewers. This easy microwave recipe is a game changer, offering an exciting twist to your regular chicken skewers, perfect for quick weeknight dinners or weekend get-togethers.

Servings: 4

Prepping Time: 15 minutes

Cook Time: 20 minutes

Difficulty: Easy

Ingredients:

- 500g boneless chicken, cut into chunks
- 2 limes, juiced
- 3 tablespoons curry powder
- 2 tablespoons honey
- Salt to taste
- 4 wooden skewers soaked in water

Step-by-Step Preparation:

1. Mix lime juice, curry powder, honey, and salt in a bowl. Add chicken pieces and marinate for 10 minutes.
2. Thread the chicken onto the skewers.
3. Place skewers on a microwave-safe dish and cook for 20 minutes at 800W, turning halfway through.
4. Ensure chicken is thoroughly cooked before serving.

Nutritional Facts: (Per serving)

- Calories: 250
- Protein: 25g
- Fat: 10g
- Carbs: 15g
- Fiber: 2g
- Sugar: 10g

Try these Grilled Curry Lime Chicken Skewers and turn your kitchen into a gourmet haven. This delicious, easy-to-make dish promises to take your taste buds on an exotic journey right in the comfort of your home. Dinner will never be the same again.

Chapter 4: Afternoon Delights for Instant Cravings

31: Cinnamon Sugar Soft Pretzels

Indulge in the simple pleasure of homemade Cinnamon Sugar Soft Pretzels, made even easier with the convenience of a microwave. An ideal snack for a cozy evening at home, these soft pretzels are seasoned with a sweet blend of cinnamon and sugar for a delightful treat.

> Servings: 6
>
> Prepping Time: 15 minutes
>
> Cook Time: 3 minutes
>
> Difficulty: Easy

Ingredients:

- 1 pack of refrigerated pizza dough
- 4 tablespoons melted unsalted butter
- 1/2 cup white sugar
- 2 teaspoons ground cinnamon

Step-by-Step Preparation:

1. Roll pizza dough into six pretzel shapes.
2. Place pretzels on a microwave-safe dish.
3. Microwave for about 3 minutes or until pretzels are cooked through.
4. Brush each pretzel with melted butter.
5. Combine sugar and cinnamon in a separate bowl and sprinkle over the buttered pretzels.
6. Allow to cool before serving.

Nutritional Facts: (Per serving)

- ❖ Calories: 220
- ❖ Fat: 6g
- ❖ Carbohydrates: 36g
- ❖ Protein: 5g
- ❖ Sugar: 10g

Relish the heavenly taste of these Cinnamon Sugar Soft Pretzels right out of your microwave. Soft, sweet, and just a bit buttery, they're perfect for a quick snack or a family dessert. Easy to make and even easier to enjoy, these pretzels are sure to become a favorite!

32: Hummus Dip With Pita Bread

Breathe a burst of health and taste into your snack time with this easy microwave Hummus Dip with Pita Bread Slices and Vegetable recipe. This Mediterranean-inspired snack, packed with protein and fiber, is ideal for any time of the day.

Servings: 4-6

Prepping Time: 15 minutes

Cook Time: 2 minutes

Difficulty: Easy

Ingredients:

- 1 can (15 oz) chickpeas
- 2 cloves garlic
- 2 tablespoons tahini
- 2 tablespoons olive oil
- Juice of 1 lemon
- Salt to taste
- 1/2 cup water
- Pita bread slices

➤ Assorted raw vegetables (carrots, celery, cucumber, etc.)

Step-by-Step Preparation:

1. Drain the chickpeas and keep the liquid aside.
2. Combine chickpeas, garlic, tahini, olive oil, lemon juice, and salt in a blender or food processor. Blend until smooth, adding the chickpea liquid or water as needed.
3. Transfer the hummus to a microwave-safe bowl and microwave for 2 minutes. Stir halfway through.
4. Serve warm with pita bread slices and assorted vegetables.

Nutritional Facts: (Per serving)

- ❖ Calories: 220
- ❖ Protein: 7g
- ❖ Carbs: 24g
- ❖ Fiber: 5g
- ❖ Fat: 11g

Revamp your snack time with this heart-healthy, easy-to-make Hummus Dip paired with Pita Bread and veggies. Ready in under 20 minutes, this dish is a feast for your taste buds and a powerhouse of essential nutrients, ensuring that your healthy eating goals stay right on track.

33: Thai Style Spicy Chicken Wings

Start your meal with a kick by trying our Thai Style Spicy Chicken Wings. This appetizer combines juicy chicken wings and spicy Thai flavors, cooked perfectly in your microwave. A simple and quick recipe; that turns your ordinary evening into a mini celebration.

Servings: 4

Prepping Time: 15 minutes

Cook Time: 20 minutes

Difficulty: Easy

Ingredients:

- 12 chicken wings
- 2 cloves of garlic, minced
- 3 tablespoons of soy sauce
- 2 tablespoons of honey
- 1 tablespoon of Sriracha sauce
- 1 teaspoon of red pepper flakes
- Salt to taste
- Chopped fresh cilantro for garnish

Step-by-Step Preparation:

1. Mix garlic, soy sauce, honey, Sriracha, red pepper flakes, and salt in a bowl.
2. Toss the chicken wings in the sauce until fully coated.
3. Place the wings in a microwave-safe dish and cook on high for 20 minutes, turning halfway through.
4. Allow to cool slightly, garnish with cilantro and serve.

Nutritional Facts: (Per serving)

- ❖ Calories: 270
- ❖ Fat: 16g
- ❖ Protein: 22g
- ❖ Carbs: 10g
- ❖ Sodium: 730mg

In conclusion, these Thai Style Spicy Chicken Wings are not just an easy microwave dish to prepare but also loaded with flavors that impress your guests. No need to order out when you can create this delicious appetizer in the comfort of your kitchen.

34: Hot Popcorn in the Microwave

Introducing your go-to recipe for a quick, crunchy, and satisfying snack - hot popcorn popped perfectly in your microwave. Ideal for movie nights, gatherings, or just a treat to keep you company in your downtime.

Servings: 4

Prepping Time: 2 minutes

Cook Time: 4 minutes

Difficulty: Easy

Ingredients:

- 1/2 cup popcorn kernels
- 1 microwave-safe bowl
- 1 microwave-safe plate (as a lid)
- Salt to taste

Step-by-Step Preparation:

1. Place the popcorn kernels into the microwave-safe bowl.
2. Cover the bowl with the microwave-safe plate.

3. Microwave the popcorn on high for 3-4 minutes or until the pops are about 2 seconds apart.
4. Carefully remove the bowl (it will be hot), let it sit for a minute, then uncover it.
5. Sprinkle with salt, stir, and serve immediately.

Nutritional Facts: (Per serving)

- Calories: 31
- Fat: 0.4g
- Carbohydrates: 6g
- Fiber: 1.2g
- Protein: 1g

Make the most of your microwave and give your family or friends a snack they'll love. This hot popcorn recipe is not only super easy and quick to make, but it also offers a healthier alternative to pre-packaged popcorn. So the next time you crave something salty and crunchy, you know what to pop in your microwave!

35: Kale Chip Covered

Kick your snack game up with our Kale Chip Covered with Melted Parmesan Cheese and Spices. This easy microwave dish is a delicious blend of crunch, flavor, and nutrition that everyone in the family will love.

Servings: 2

Prepping Time: 5 minutes

Cook Time: 2-3 minutes

Difficulty: Easy

Ingredients:

- 2 cups of kale, torn into bite-sized pieces
- 2 tablespoons of olive oil
- 1/2 cup of grated parmesan cheese
- 1 teaspoon of garlic powder
- Salt and pepper to taste

Step-by-Step Preparation:

1. Wash and dry kale thoroughly.
2. Toss kale in olive oil, ensuring every piece is coated.

3. Spread kale on a microwave-safe plate.
4. Sprinkle-grated parmesan, garlic powder, salt, and pepper over the kale.
5. Microwave for 2-3 minutes or until the edges of the kale are brown and crispy. Observe to avoid burning.

Nutritional Facts: (Per serving)

- Calories: 230
- Fat: 17g
- Carbohydrates: 10g
- Protein: 9g
- Dietary fiber: 3g

Embrace the delight of homemade kale chips covered with melted parmesan cheese and spices. Savor the crunch, taste the cheesiness, and enjoy the burst of flavor in every bite. Say goodbye to store-bought snacks and make your own in minutes, right in the microwave!

36: Italian Pizzette Mini Pizza Bites

Immerse yourself in the delectable flavors of Italy with this bite-sized Italian Pizzette. Perfect as an appetizer or a snack, these mini pizza bites are topped with various assorted ingredients to tantalize your taste buds. Plus, they're an easy microwave dish!

> Servings: 4
>
> Prepping Time: 20 minutes
>
> Cook Time: 5 minutes
>
> Difficulty: Easy

Ingredients:

> - 4 pita bread rounds
> - 1 cup marinara sauce
> - 1 cup shredded mozzarella
> - Assorted toppings: sliced olives, chopped bell peppers, mushrooms, sliced tomatoes
> - Fresh basil for garnish

Step-by-Step Preparation:

1. Cut each pita bread into small bite-sized pieces.
2. Spread a thin layer of marinara sauce on each piece.
3. Sprinkle mozzarella cheese evenly across the pita pieces.
4. Add your desired toppings.
5. Place the pita pieces in the microwave and cook for 5 minutes or until the cheese is melted.
6. Garnish with fresh basil and serve.

Nutritional Facts: (Per serving)

- Calories: 230
- Total Fat: 9g
- Carbohydrates: 30g
- Protein: 10g

Discover the joys of Italian cuisine in a bite-sized package! These Pizzette Mini Pizza Bites are flavorful and incredibly easy to prepare. Whether you're hosting a party or just looking for a quick snack, they will become a favorite!

37: Creamy Avocado Dip With Cilantro

Enjoy the creamy, tangy, and refreshing flavor of this easy-to-make Creamy Avocado Dip with Cilantro and Lime. Perfect for an afternoon snack or a fun appetizer at parties, it's a recipe that pleases every palate and fits every occasion.

Servings: 4-6

Prepping Time: 10 Minutes

Cook Time: 2 Minutes

Difficulty: Easy

Ingredients:

- 2 ripe avocados, peeled and pitted
- Juice of 1 lime
- 2 cloves of garlic, minced
- 1/2 cup fresh cilantro, chopped
- 1/2 cup Greek yogurt
- Salt and pepper to taste

Step-by-Step Preparation:

1. Combine avocados, lime juice, minced garlic, chopped cilantro, and Greek yogurt in a blender.
2. Blend until smooth and creamy.
3. Season with salt and pepper to taste.
4. Transfer the dip to a microwave-safe bowl and microwave for 2 minutes on high.
5. Serve immediately with your favorite tortilla chips or vegetable sticks.

Nutritional Facts: (Per serving)

- ❖ Calories: 160
- ❖ Protein: 3g
- ❖ Carbohydrates: 9g
- ❖ Fat: 14g
- ❖ Fiber: 7g
- ❖ Sugar: 1g

Indulge in the freshness of avocados combined with the tang of lime and the aroma of cilantro. This Creamy Avocado Dip is not just a tasty delight; it's also a healthy option packed with beneficial fats and fibers. It's perfect for those looking for a quick and nutritious addition to their snack repertoire.

38: S'More Dip Cookies Chocolate and Marshmallow

Enjoy the nostalgic campfire flavors in the comfort of your kitchen with these easy-to-make S'More Dip Cookies! These cookies are perfect for a fun family treat or a potluck dessert.

Servings: 6

Prepping Time: 15 minutes

Cook Time: 3 minutes

Difficulty: Easy

Ingredients:

- 1 cup Semi-Sweet Chocolate Chips
- 2 cups Mini Marshmallows
- 1/2 cup Heavy Cream
- 1 pack of Graham Crackers
- 1/2 tsp Vanilla Extract

Step-by-Step Preparation:

1. In a microwave-safe bowl, combine the chocolate chips and heavy cream. Microwave for 30 seconds, then stir until smooth.
2. Stir in the vanilla extract.
3. Spread the chocolate mixture on the graham crackers.
4. Top with marshmallows.
5. Microwave on high for 1 minute or until the marshmallows are puffed and golden.
6. Allow to cool before serving.

Nutritional Facts: (Per serving)

- Calories: 300
- Fat: 15g
- Protein: 2g
- Carbohydrates: 40g
- Sugar: 30g

Bring the outdoors indoors with this easy and delectable S'More Dip Cookies recipe. Ready in under 20 minutes, these delicious cookies deliver the classic s'mores taste without needing a campfire. They're perfect for those sweet tooth cravings or sharing at your next gathering.

39: Bacon Stuffed Mushroom Caps

Discover the joy of these bite-sized wonders - Bacon Stuffed Mushroom Caps with Spinach. A delightful blend of crispy bacon, succulent mushrooms, and fresh spinach, this easy-to-make microwave recipe promises to deliver incredible flavors right to your dining table.

Servings: 4

Prepping Time: 15 Minutes

Cook Time: 10 Minutes

Difficulty: Easy

Ingredients:

- 12 large white mushrooms
- 6 slices of bacon
- 2 cups of fresh spinach, washed and chopped
- 1 cup of grated cheddar cheese
- Salt and pepper to taste

Step-by-Step Preparation:

1. Rinse the mushrooms and remove the stems. Set aside.

2. In a microwave-safe bowl, cook bacon for 5 minutes or until crispy.
3. Mix the cooked bacon, spinach, and cheese in a bowl.
4. Fill the mushroom caps with the bacon-spinach mixture.
5. Place the stuffed mushrooms on a microwave-safe plate and cook for 5 minutes or until the cheese is bubbly.

Nutritional Facts: (Per serving)

- ❖ Calories: 220
- ❖ Total Fat: 14g
- ❖ Protein: 12g
- ❖ Carbohydrates: 8g
- ❖ Fiber: 2g

Indulge in these savory Bacon Stuffed Mushroom Caps with Spinach - an enchanting taste experience that's both satisfying and nutritious. Perfect as an appetizer, side dish, or light main, this dish makes cooking a breeze without compromising taste or health. Enjoy!

40: Caramelized Corn Cakes

Delight in the simple, healthy, and delicious Caramelized Corn Cakes Puffed Whole Grain Crispbread recipe. These crispbreads, cooked in a microwave, offer an ideal snack or creative addition to any meal.

Servings: 4

Prepping Time: 10 minutes

Cook Time: 5 minutes

Difficulty: Easy

Ingredients:

- 4 whole grain crispbreads
- 1 cup corn kernels
- 2 tablespoons brown sugar
- 1 tablespoon olive oil
- Pinch of salt

Step-by-Step Preparation:

1. Mix corn kernels, brown sugar, and olive oil in a bowl.
2. Spread the mixture evenly over the crispbreads.

3. Place the crispbreads in the microwave, and cook on high for 5 minutes or until the corn kernels caramelize.
4. Let them cool before serving.

Nutritional Facts: (Per serving)

- Calories: 180 kcal
- Protein: 4g
- Carbs: 30g
- Fat: 6g
- Fiber: 5g
- Sugar: 7g

Enjoy the delightful crunch of these Caramelized Corn Cakes, Puffed Whole Grain Crispbreads. Quick to prepare and packed with nutrients, they are perfect for a snack, appetizer, or part of a light lunch. Savor the balance of sweet caramelized corn and the hearty whole-grain crispbread in every bite.

Chapter 5: Dashing Dinners Done in Jiffy

41: Pesto Chicken Fettuccini

Savor a mouthwatering Italian dish at home with this easy Pesto Chicken Fettuccine with Cherry Tomatoes recipe. You can microwave this delicious pasta meal without breaking a sweat. Perfect for a weeknight dinner or casual get-together.

Servings: 4

Prepping Time: 10 minutes

Cook Time: 20 minutes

Difficulty: Easy

Ingredients:

- 2 boneless chicken breasts, cubed
- 2 cups of fettuccine pasta
- 1 cup of basil pesto
- 1 cup of cherry tomatoes, halved
- 1 cup of grated Parmesan cheese

- ➢ Salt and pepper to taste

Step-by-Step Preparation:

1. Cook fettuccine in the microwave according to package instructions.
2. In a microwave-safe bowl, cook the chicken cubes for 6-7 minutes until cooked.
3. Add pesto and cherry tomatoes to the chicken. Mix well and microwave for 2 minutes.
4. Combine the cooked pasta with the chicken mixture. Add Parmesan, salt, and pepper. Stir well.
5. Serve immediately while hot.

Nutritional Facts: (Per serving)

- ❖ Calories: 520
- ❖ Protein: 30g
- ❖ Fat: 22g
- ❖ Carbohydrates: 50g
- ❖ Dietary Fiber: 3g
- ❖ Sugars: 4g

Savor the delightful blend of fresh basil, tangy cherry tomatoes, succulent chicken, and al dente fettuccine. This Pesto Chicken Fettuccine with Cherry Tomatoes recipe will impress with its simplicity and gourmet taste. Enjoy a touch of Italy in your kitchen any day of the week.

42: Whole Wheat Pasta With Vegetables

Unleash your inner chef with this quick and healthy Whole Wheat Pasta with Vegetable recipe. It's ideal for a wholesome lunch or dinner, packed with fiber, vitamins, and nutrients while maintaining an irresistible taste.

> **Servings:** 4
>
> **Prepping Time:** 15 minutes
>
> **Cook Time:** 10 minutes
>
> **Difficulty:** Easy

Ingredients:

- 2 cups whole wheat pasta
- 1 bell pepper, sliced
- 1 zucchini, sliced
- 2 carrots, diced
- 2 tablespoons olive oil
- 1 garlic clove, minced
- Salt and pepper to taste

Step-by-Step Preparation:

1. Cook the pasta according to package instructions and drain.
2. Place the vegetables, olive oil, garlic, salt, and pepper in a microwave-safe bowl, mixing them well.
3. Cover the bowl and microwave for 5-7 minutes until the vegetables are tender.
4. Combine the cooked pasta and vegetables, tossing well to combine.
5. Serve immediately and enjoy!

Nutritional Facts: (Per serving)

- Calories: 320
- Fat: 8g
- Protein: 12g
- Fiber: 8g
- Carbohydrates: 52g

Embrace the ease of microwave cooking and the goodness of whole grains with this Whole Wheat Pasta with Vegetable recipe. It's a versatile dish you can tweak with your favorite veggies and spices. The perfect blend of health and flavor right on your plate!

43: Classic Caesar Salad With Grilled Chicken Fillet

Experience the delight of the classic Caesar Salad with an added twist of succulent grilled chicken fillet. This dish is more than just light and nutritious. It's straightforward to prepare in your microwave, perfect for a quick lunch or dinner.

> Servings: 4
>
> Prepping Time: 10 minutes
>
> Cook Time: 5 minutes
>
> Difficulty: Easy

Ingredients:

- 4 boneless, skinless chicken fillets
- 1 head of romaine lettuce
- 1/2 cup of grated Parmesan cheese
- 1 cup of croutons
- 2 cloves of garlic, minced
- Caesar salad dressing
- Salt and pepper to taste

Step-by-Step Preparation:

1. Season the chicken fillets with salt, pepper, and minced garlic.
2. Place the seasoned fillets in the microwave on a microwave-safe dish, and cook for about 5 minutes or until cooked through.
3. In the meantime, chop the romaine lettuce, mix in the croutons, and sprinkle the Parmesan cheese.
4. Once the chicken is cooked, slice it into strips and add it to the salad.
5. Drizzle your Caesar salad dressing over the top, toss well, and serve.

Nutritional Facts: (Per serving)

- Calories: 350
- Protein: 28g
- Fat: 18g
- Carbs: 15g
- Fiber: 3g
- Sugar: 3g

Indulge in this delectable Classic Caesar Salad with Grilled Chicken Fillet. Packed with flavors, it is a perfect blend of crisp, creamy, and savory elements that will satisfy your taste buds. It's quick, simple, and ideal for healthy yet delicious meals.

44: Eggplant Parmigiana

Welcome to the world of easy and delicious cooking! Prepare to prepare Eggplant Parmigiana in your kitchen, a classic Italian dish. Even if you're a beginner, our microwave recipe ensures this comforting meal is just a few steps away.

>Servings: 4
>
>Prepping Time: 15 minutes
>
>Cook Time: 15 minutes
>
>Difficulty: Easy

Ingredients:

- 2 large eggplants, sliced into 1/2-inch rounds
- 2 cups marinara sauce
- 2 cups shredded mozzarella cheese
- 1 cup grated Parmesan cheese
- 1/2 cup fresh basil leaves
- Salt and pepper to taste

Step-by-Step Preparation:

1. Arrange eggplant slices in a microwave-safe dish, season with salt and pepper.
2. Top with marinara sauce, mozzarella, and Parmesan cheese.
3. Cover the dish with microwave-safe plastic wrap.
4. Microwave on high for about 15 minutes until the eggplant is tender and the cheese is melted and slightly browned.
5. Garnish with fresh basil leaves before serving.

Nutritional Facts: (Per serving)

- ❖ Calories: 275
- ❖ Fat: 16g
- ❖ Carbohydrates: 20g
- ❖ Protein: 17g
- ❖ Fiber: 6g
- ❖ Sodium: 800mg

In just 30 minutes, you've created a mouthwatering Eggplant Parmigiana in your microwave. Simple and delightful, this recipe gives you a taste of Italy without much effort. Perfect for a weeknight dinner or a hearty side dish, it's a tasty reminder that great cooking is within everyone's reach.

45: Sweet Potato Stuffed

Delight your senses with a healthy yet hearty, Low-Fat Whole Baked Sweet Potato Stuffed with Chicken Breast. This microwave recipe is quick and easy, providing a balanced mix of lean protein and complex carbs that taste like comfort food.

Servings: 2

Prepping Time: 10 minutes

Cook Time: 15 minutes

Difficulty: Easy

Ingredients:

- 2 medium-sized sweet potatoes
- 2 skinless, boneless chicken breasts
- 1 teaspoon of olive oil
- Salt and pepper to taste
- 2 tablespoons of low-fat Greek yogurt
- Fresh herbs for garnish

Step-by-Step Preparation:

1. Clean the sweet potatoes, then pierce them with a fork several times.
2. Microwave the sweet potatoes on high for 5-7 minutes until tender.
3. While the potatoes are cooking, season the chicken with salt, pepper, and oil, then microwave for 6-8 minutes until cooked thoroughly.
4. Allow both to cool slightly, then slice the potatoes open and fluff the insides with a fork.
5. Dice the cooked chicken and mix it with Greek yogurt.
6. Stuff each potato with the chicken mixture, garnish with fresh herbs and serve.

Nutritional Facts: (Per serving)

- Calories: 380 kcal
- Protein: 45g
- Carbohydrates: 40g
- Fat: 5g
- Fiber: 7g
- Sodium: 250mg

Indulge in this simple, nutritious recipe that beautifully combines the sweet, earthy flavors of the sweet potato with lean, flavorful chicken breast. Perfect for a quick lunch or an after-workout meal, it's an easy way to satisfy your palate while caring for your health.

46: Turkey Meatballs With Zucchini Noodles

Enjoy a healthy, flavorful twist on a classic with these Turkey Meatballs served over Zucchini Noodles. This easy microwave dish is a high-protein, low-carb alternative to pasta that will satisfy you without guilt.

Servings: 4

Prepping Time: 20 Minutes

Cook Time: 10 Minutes

Difficulty: Easy

Ingredients:

- 1 lb ground turkey
- 1/4 cup breadcrumbs
- 1/4 cup Parmesan cheese
- 1 egg
- 2 cloves garlic, minced
- 1/4 cup chopped parsley
- Salt and pepper to taste
- 4 medium zucchinis, spiralized
- 1 cup marinara sauce

Step-by-Step Preparation:

1. Mix turkey, breadcrumbs, Parmesan, egg, garlic, parsley, salt, and pepper in a bowl.
2. Form mixture into meatballs and place in a microwave-safe dish.
3. Microwave meatballs for 6-7 minutes until fully cooked.
4. Meanwhile, place spiralized zucchini in a microwave-safe word and cook for 2-3 minutes until tender.
5. Heat marinara sauce in the microwave.
6. Serve meatballs over zucchini noodles and top with warm marinara sauce.

Nutritional Facts: (Per serving)

- ❖ Calories: 320
- ❖ Protein: 30g
- ❖ Carbohydrates: 20g
- ❖ Fat: 12g
- ❖ Fiber: 3g
- ❖ Sugar: 7g

Enjoy these delightful Turkey Meatballs with Zucchini Noodles as a quick, nutritious meal. Perfect for those busy weeknights, this microwave dish saves time and offers a delicious way to incorporate more veggies into your diet.

47: Garlic King Prawn Wood Fired Pizza

Welcome to a delightful combination of flavor and simplicity - Garlic King Prawn Wood Fired Pizza. With a crunchy base, succulent prawns, and aromatic garlic, this recipe brings a new twist to your regular pizza, using a microwave to achieve that wood-fired flavor in the comfort of your home.

Servings: 2

Prepping Time: 15 Minutes

Cook Time: 10 Minutes

Difficulty: Easy

Ingredients:

- 1 pizza base
- 150 grams of king prawns, peeled and deveined
- 2 tablespoons of olive oil
- 2 cloves of garlic, minced
- 100 grams of mozzarella cheese
- 1 tablespoon of dried oregano
- 1/2 cup of tomato sauce
- Salt and pepper to taste

Step-by-Step Preparation:

1. Preheat your microwave to its highest setting.
2. On the pizza base, spread the tomato sauce evenly.
3. Heat the olive oil and sauté the garlic and prawns in a pan until they turn pink. Season with salt, pepper, and oregano.
4. Spread the prawn mixture on the pizza base and sprinkle with mozzarella cheese.
5. Cook the pizza in the microwave for about 10 minutes or until the cheese is bubbling and slightly golden.

Nutritional Facts: (Per serving)

- ❖ Calories: 450
- ❖ Protein: 25 grams
- ❖ Fat: 20 grams
- ❖ Carbohydrates: 50 grams
- ❖ Sodium: 850 milligrams

A bite into this Garlic King Prawn Wood Fired Pizza will transport you to an Italian trattoria. The delectable seafood taste blends perfectly with the traditional pizza ingredients. It's a quick, easy, and flavorful option to impress your friends or to make any evening more special. Enjoy this unique fusion of sea and land at your next dinner!

48: Hearty Sausage Casserole

Experience the taste of home in your kitchen with this Hearty Sausage Casserole with Floating Sausage. A perfect microwave dish that's hearty, simple, and incredibly delicious, guaranteed to become your new family favorite.

> Servings: 4
>
> **Prepping Time:** 10 minutes
>
> **Cook Time:** 20 minutes
>
> **Difficulty:** Easy

Ingredients:

- 8 good quality pork sausages
- 2 cans of baked beans
- 1 can diced tomatoes
- 1 chopped onion
- 2 cloves garlic, minced
- 1 tsp paprika
- Salt and pepper to taste

Step-by-Step Preparation:

1. In a microwave-safe dish, place the sausages and cook on high for 3 minutes.
2. Remove the links, add the onion and garlic, and microwave for 2 minutes.
3. Add the canned beans, diced tomatoes, paprika, and season with salt and pepper. Stir well.
4. Nestle the sausages on top and microwave on high for 15 minutes.
5. Let it stand for 2 minutes before serving.

Nutritional Facts: (Per serving)

- ❖ Calories: 435
- ❖ Protein: 21g
- ❖ Carbohydrates: 33g
- ❖ Fat: 25g
- ❖ Fiber: 9g

Bid farewell to time-consuming recipes without compromising the richness and heartiness of your meal. This Hearty Sausage Casserole with Floating Sausage makes an ideal dish for a quick weeknight dinner or a lazy weekend brunch, providing comfort in every bite. Enjoy the simplicity without sacrificing taste or quality.

49: Grilled Salmon Steak

This easy yet satisfying grilled salmon steak recipe takes your culinary skills to the next level. Perfect for those quick and healthy meals, this dish bursts with flavor and essential nutrients, cooked to perfection in your microwave.

Servings: 2

Prepping Time: 15 minutes

Cook Time: 6 minutes

Difficulty: Easy

Ingredients:

- 2 fresh salmon steaks
- 2 tablespoons olive oil
- Salt and pepper to taste
- 1 lemon
- Fresh dill for garnish

Step-by-Step Preparation:

1. Rinse the salmon steaks and pat dry.

2. Drizzle olive oil on both sides of the salmon, then season with salt and pepper.
3. Place the steaks on a microwave-safe dish.
4. Squeeze the lemon over the salmon.
5. Microwave on high for 6 minutes or until the salmon is cooked through.
6. Garnish with fresh dill before serving.

Nutritional Facts: (Per serving)

- ❖ Calories: 368
- ❖ Fat: 23g
- ❖ Protein: 34g
- ❖ Carbohydrates: 2g
- ❖ Fiber: 0g
- ❖ Sugar: 1g

Dive into a journey of flavors with this easy microwave Grilled Salmon Steak recipe. It's an ideal dish to whip up on busy days, nourishing you without sacrificing taste. The minimal prep time and easy cooking steps make it a perfect meal for novice and experienced cooks alike.

50: Fried Tofu With Sesame Seeds

Discover the harmony of textures and flavors in this quick and easy "Fried Tofu with Sesame Seeds" recipe. This will surely tickle your taste buds, perfect for those seeking a vegan option or simply a delicious dish.

> **Servings:** 4
>
> **Prepping Time:** 10 minutes
>
> **Cook Time:** 3 minutes
>
> **Difficulty:** Easy

Ingredients:

- ➢ 400g firm tofu
- ➢ 2 tablespoons soy sauce
- ➢ 1 tablespoon sesame oil
- ➢ 2 tablespoons sesame seeds
- ➢ Spring onions for garnish

Step-by-Step Preparation:

1. Cut the tofu into cubes and pat dry.
2. Drizzle with soy sauce and sesame oil.

3. Sprinkle with sesame seeds, ensuring each cube is evenly coated.
4. Place in a microwave-safe dish and microwave for 3 minutes.
5. Garnish with spring onions and serve hot.

Nutritional Facts: (Per serving)

- ❖ Calories: 180
- ❖ Protein: 12g
- ❖ Carbohydrates: 5g
- ❖ Fat: 13g
- ❖ Fiber: 2g

End your meal on a high note with this crispy, flavorful "Fried Tofu with Sesame Seeds." Easy to prepare in the microwave, it's the perfect dish for busy weeknights or when you want something quick, healthy, and satisfying.

Chapter 6: Midnight Munchies for the Night Owls

51: Cheesy Breadsticks

Dive into the delightful experience of homemade Cheesy Breadsticks with a tangy marinara dip using your microwave! This recipe is perfect for quick snacks, surprise guests, or for that cheesy comfort.

Servings: 2-3

Prepping Time: 10 minutes

Cook Time: 5 minutes

Difficulty: Easy

Ingredients:

- 1 pre-made pizza dough
- 1 cup shredded mozzarella cheese
- 2 tablespoons olive oil
- 1 teaspoon garlic powder
- 1 teaspoon dried oregano

- Salt to taste
- 1 cup marinara sauce for dipping

Step-by-Step Preparation:

1. Roll out the pizza dough into a rectangular shape and place it on a microwave-safe dish.
2. Brush dough with olive oil, then sprinkle with garlic powder, oregano, and salt.
3. Evenly distribute shredded cheese over the dough.
4. Microwave for 4-5 minutes or until cheese is melted and bubbly.
5. Slice into sticks and serve hot with marinara sauce for dipping.

Nutritional Facts: (Per serving)

- Calories: 350
- Fat: 15g
- Carbohydrates: 40g
- Protein: 15g
- Sodium: 850mg

This Cheesy Breadstick with Marinara Sauce recipe will surely win over your tastebuds. It's an effortlessly delicious dish you can whip up anytime. Enjoy it while watching a movie, having a catch-up session with friends, or craving some cheesy goodness - it's satisfaction in every bite!

52: Chocolate Mug Cakes

Get your chocolate fix quickly with these easy-to-make, gooey Chocolate Mug Cakes. Ready in just a few minutes, these personal-sized treats are perfect for late-night cravings, quick desserts, or when you need a small indulgence.

Servings: 2

Prepping Time: 3 minutes

Cook Time: 2 minutes

Difficulty: Easy

Ingredients:

- 4 tablespoons all-purpose flour
- 4 tablespoons granulated sugar
- 2 tablespoons unsweetened cocoa powder
- 1/8 teaspoon baking powder
- a pinch of salt
- 3 tablespoons milk
- 2 tablespoons vegetable oil
- 1/4 teaspoon pure vanilla extract

Step-by-Step Preparation:

1. In a medium bowl, whisk together the dry ingredients.
2. Stir in the milk, vegetable oil, and vanilla until smooth.
3. Divide the mixture between two microwave-safe mugs.
4. Microwave each cup separately for about 90 seconds on high or until the cake rises and is set in the middle.
5. Let cool for a minute before eating.

Nutritional Facts: (Per serving)

- Calories: 370
- Fat: 18g
- Carbs: 50g
- Protein: 4g
- Sugar: 30g

Satisfy your sweet tooth without fuss with these Chocolate Mug Cakes. This quick and easy recipe is perfect for any time you need something special but need more time and desire to bake a whole cake. Enjoy the decadent, rich flavor in just a matter of minutes.

53: Energy Protein Balls

They are introducing Energy Protein Balls - a quick, nutritious snack to satisfy cravings and boost protein. Easy to make in the microwave, these balls are filled with nuts, seeds, and oats, delivering a hearty energy punch.

Servings: 12 Balls

Prepping Time: 10 Minutes

Cook Time: 2 Minutes

Difficulty: Easy

Ingredients:

- 1 cup rolled oats
- 1/2 cup almond butter
- 1/4 cup honey
- 1/2 cup chocolate protein powder
- 1/4 cup chia seeds
- 1/4 cup flax seeds

Step-by-Step Preparation:

1. Combine all ingredients in a bowl and mix well.

2. Roll into 1-inch balls.
3. Place on a microwave-safe dish and microwave for 2 minutes.
4. Let cool before consuming.

Nutritional Facts: (Per serving)

- Calories: 190 kcal
- Protein: 10g
- Carbs: 22g
- Fat: 7g
- Fiber: 4g

These Energy Protein Balls are the perfect grab-and-go snack, ideal for post-workout recovery or to curb mid-afternoon hunger. They will become a favorite in your healthy snack repertoire and are easy to make, delicious to eat, and packed with nutrients.

54: Healthy Trail Mix Snack

Welcome to a quick and easy microwave recipe that is nutritious and delicious! This homemade Healthy Trail Mix Snack will be your new favorite companion for a midday munch or a post-workout snack, providing just the right combination of sweet, salty, and nutty flavors.

Servings: 10

Prepping Time: 10 minutes

Cook Time: 2 minutes

Difficulty: Easy

Ingredients:

- 1 cup almonds
- 1/2 cup pumpkin seeds
- 1/2 cup dried cranberries
- 1/2 cup chocolate chips
- 1/2 cup dried apricots
- 1/2 cup raisins

Step-by-Step Preparation:

1. Mix all the ingredients in a large bowl.
2. Microwave the mix on high for 2 minutes, stirring halfway through.
3. Allow it to cool before serving.

Nutritional Facts: (Per serving)

- Calories: 200
- Protein: 6g
- Fat: 12g
- Carbohydrates: 22g
- Fiber: 3g
- Sugar: 14g

In no time at all, you have a Healthy Trail Mix Snack that's ready to take with you wherever you go. It's more than just a simple, fast, and convenient snack. It's also loaded with good-for-you nutrients that will keep you fueled and satisfied all day. Enjoy it during your outdoor adventures or simply as a healthier snack option at work. Happy munching!

55: Pepperoni Mini Pizza Bagels

Delight your taste buds with these bite-sized Pepperoni Mini Pizza Bagels. An easy microwave recipe that transforms simple ingredients into a snack-time favorite that both kids and adults will love. Enjoy the satisfying crunch and cheesy goodness in less than 15 minutes!

Servings: 4

Prepping Time: 5 Minutes

Cook Time: 10 Minutes

Difficulty: Easy

Ingredients:

- 8 mini bagels, halved
- 1 cup pizza sauce
- 2 cups shredded mozzarella cheese
- 1/2 cup mini pepperoni

Step-by-Step Preparation:

1. Arrange bagel halves on a microwave-safe plate.

2. Spread each bagel half with pizza sauce, sprinkle mozzarella, and top with mini pepperoni.
3. Microwave for 1-2 minutes on high or until cheese is melted and bubbly. Allow to cool for a minute before serving.

Nutritional Facts: (Per serving)

- Calories: 350 kcal
- Protein: 15 g
- Carbohydrates: 45 g
- Fat: 14 g
- Sodium: 700 mg
- Fiber: 3 g

These Pepperoni Mini Pizza Bagels are the perfect blend of comfort and convenience. These delicious bite-sized pizzas serve as an excellent appetizer for gatherings or a quick fix for sudden hunger pangs. Enjoy the process and the product of this easy recipe!

56: Organic Apple Cinnamon Chips

Embrace a healthier snacking alternative with these delightful Organic Apple Cinnamon Chips. These chips offer a sweet and crispy satisfaction to curb your midday cravings.

Servings: 2

Prepping Time: 10 minutes

Cook Time: 5-6 minutes

Difficulty: Easy

Ingredients:

- 2 large organic apples
- 1 tsp cinnamon powder

Step-by-Step Preparation:

1. Thinly slice the apples, ensuring uniformity for even cooking.
2. Sprinkle the slices with cinnamon, ensuring each piece is well coated.
3. Place the apple slices in a single layer on a microwave-safe plate.

4. Microwave for 5-6 minutes, checking every minute after the third minute to avoid burning.
5. Allow to cool, and then enjoy your crispy apple cinnamon chips!

Nutritional Facts: (Per serving)

- Calories: 95 kcal
- Carbohydrates: 25g
- Fiber: 5g
- Sugar: 18g
- Vitamin C: 10mg

End your hunt for the perfect guilt-free snack with these Organic Apple Cinnamon Chips. Not only are they a breeze to prepare, but they also provide a fantastic way to use surplus apples. Enjoy a delicious, healthy treat anytime, anywhere!

57: Hot Chocolate With Salted Caramel

Indulge in the warmth of a mug of Hot Chocolate with Salted Caramel, perfect for chilly evenings. This cozy concoction elevates the classic hot cocoa with a hint of luxurious salted caramel. It's not just a drink; it's an experience you can create within minutes using your microwave.

Servings: 2

Prepping Time: 5 minutes

Cook Time: 2 minutes

Difficulty: Easy

Ingredients:

- 2 cups of milk
- 4 tablespoons of cocoa powder
- 4 tablespoons of sugar
- 1/4 teaspoon of salt
- 4 tablespoons of store-bought salted caramel sauce

Step-by-Step Preparation:

1. Combine milk, cocoa powder, sugar, and salt in a microwave-safe bowl.
2. Heat the mixture in the microwave for 2 minutes.
3. Stir in the salted caramel sauce.
4. Divide the hot chocolate between two mugs and serve warm.

Nutritional Facts: (Per serving)

- Calories: 265
- Protein: 8g
- Carbohydrates: 40g
- Fat: 10g
- Sodium: 390mg

Relish the decadence of Hot Chocolate with Salted Caramel in the comfort of your home. Quick, easy, and made with readily available ingredients, this sweet treat promises to be a hit with kids and adults alike. Perfect for a quiet night in or a festive celebration - it's the magic of hot chocolate, made even better.

58: Roasted Chickpeas

Welcome to a culinary adventure that's healthy, simple, and delicious! "Roasted Chickpeas with Smoked Paprika" is an easy microwave recipe that combines rich, smoky flavors with the wholesome goodness of chickpeas - perfect for a guilt-free snack or an exciting salad topper.

Servings: 4

Prepping Time: 10 minutes

Cook Time: 15 minutes

Difficulty: Easy

Ingredients:

- 2 cups canned chickpeas, drained and rinsed
- 1 tablespoon olive oil
- 1 teaspoon smoked paprika
- Salt to taste

Step-by-Step Preparation:

1. Rinse and dry the chickpeas thoroughly.
2. Combine chickpeas, olive oil, smoked paprika, and salt in a bowl.

3. Transfer the mixture to a microwave-safe dish.
4. Microwave on high for 15 minutes, pausing every 5 minutes to stir.
5. Let cool before serving.

Nutritional Facts: (Per serving)

- Calories: 180
- Protein: 7g
- Fat: 7g
- Carbohydrates: 23g
- Fiber: 5g
- Sodium: 300mg

And there you have it - the Roasted Chickpeas with Smoked Paprika. This easy-to-make microwave recipe will satiate your cravings without sacrificing health. It's a delightful snack and versatile addition to salads, soups, and grain bowls. Enjoy this culinary masterpiece and let your taste buds revel in the magic of healthy, tasty simplicity.

59: Rustic Potato Skins With Cheese

Indulge in these delicious, crispy, Rustic Potato Skins filled with melting cheese! They're a perfect appetizer or snack, serving the essence of comfort food in each bite. This microwave recipe is convenient, easy to follow, and a sure delight for all potato lovers.

Servings: 4

Prepping Time: 15 minutes

Cook Time: 10 minutes

Difficulty: Easy

Ingredients:

- 4 large potatoes
- 1 cup shredded cheddar cheese
- 4 strips of bacon, cooked and crumbled
- 2 green onions, chopped
- Sour cream for serving
- Salt and pepper to taste

Step-by-Step Preparation:

1. Scrub potatoes clean and pierce with a fork. Microwave on high for about 10 minutes or until soft.
2. Allow potatoes to cool, cut in half lengthwise, then scoop out the flesh leaving a ¼ inch layer of potato on the skin.
3. Sprinkle the insides with cheese, bacon, salt, and pepper.
4. Microwave again for about 1-2 minutes until the cheese is melted.
5. Garnish with green onions and serve with a dollop of sour cream.

Nutritional Facts: (Per serving)

- Calories: 265
- Protein: 12g
- Carbohydrates: 28g
- Fat: 12g
- Sodium: 370mg
- Fiber: 3g

Dive into these Rustic Potato Skins with Cheese and experience the irresistible combination of crunchy skins and oozy cheese. It's a perfect dish for any gathering, allowing you to enjoy a restaurant-like treat at home. Quick, easy, and deliciously satisfying!

60: Baked Orange Sweet Potato Fries

Introduce a burst of sweet citrus with these delightful Baked Orange Sweet Potato Fries. This easy microwave recipe offers a compelling balance of flavors and is a perfect side for family dinners or casual gatherings.

Servings: 4

Prepping Time: 10 minutes

Cook Time: 15 minutes

Difficulty: Easy

Ingredients:

- 2 large sweet potatoes
- 2 tablespoons of olive oil
- Zest and juice of 1 orange
- Salt to taste
- 1/4 teaspoon of paprika
- 2 tablespoons of chopped fresh parsley

Step-by-Step Preparation:

1. Scrub the sweet potatoes clean, then slice them into fries.

2. Mix the orange zest, juice, olive oil, salt, and paprika in a bowl.
3. Toss the sweet potato fries in this mixture until well coated.
4. Arrange the fries on a microwave-safe plate.
5. Microwave on high for 10 minutes, then let them stand for 5 minutes to crisp up.
6. Sprinkle with parsley before serving.

Nutritional Facts: (Per serving)

- Calories: 215
- Carbohydrates: 30g
- Protein: 2.1g
- Fat: 9.7g
- Fiber: 4g
- Sugar: 9.2g

End your meal on a high note with these scrumptious Baked Orange Sweet Potato Fries. They're not just a treat for the palate; their vibrant orange hue adds color to your table. Simple to prepare, these fries are a great way to elevate your everyday meals. Enjoy their delectable crunch and citrusy tang!

Chapter 7: Seafood Splendors Straight from Microwave

61: Fried Butter Garlic Shrimp

Indulge in the aromatic delight of Fried Butter Garlic Shrimp. This microwave-friendly dish perfectly combines the buttery goodness of shrimp with the spicy tang of garlic, bringing to life an easy-to-make yet flavorful delicacy right in your kitchen.

Servings: 4

Prepping Time: 15 Minutes

Cook Time: 5 Minutes

Difficulty: Easy

Ingredients:

- 500g Shrimp, peeled and deveined
- 4 Garlic cloves, minced
- 4 tablespoons Butter
- Salt to taste

- ➢ 1 tablespoon freshly chopped Parsley
- ➢ 1/2 Lemon

Step-by-Step Preparation:

1. In a microwave-safe bowl, melt the butter.
2. Add the minced garlic to the melted butter, stirring to combine.
3. Add the shrimp to the bowl, tossing to ensure each shrimp is well coated.
4. Season with salt and microwave on high for 5 minutes or until shrimp is pink.
5. Squeeze fresh lemon juice over the cooked shrimp and garnish with chopped parsley.

Nutritional Facts: (Per serving)

- ❖ Calories: 235
- ❖ Protein: 24g
- ❖ Fat: 14g
- ❖ Carbohydrates: 2g
- ❖ Fiber: 0g
- ❖ Sugar: 0g

Savor the mouthwatering taste of Fried Butter Garlic Shrimp, an exquisite dish you can whip up in your microwave in under 20 minutes. This light and luscious meal satisfies your cravings and provides a nutrient-rich treat. Whether a quick lunch or a delightful dinner, this recipe will win hearts.

62: Chinese Seafood Medley of Shrimp

Immerse yourself in the exotic taste of the East with this easy-to-make Chinese Seafood Medley of Shrimp. Cooked in a microwave, it combines various seafood into a vibrant, tangy, and sumptuous meal.

Servings: 4

Prepping Time: 15 minutes

Cook Time: 10 minutes

Difficulty: Easy

Ingredients:

- 1 pound of shrimp, peeled and deveined
- 1/2 cup of mixed bell peppers, sliced
- 1/2 cup of baby corn, sliced
- 2 tablespoons of soy sauce
- 1 tablespoon of oyster sauce
- 1 tablespoon of cornstarch
- 2 garlic cloves, minced
- Salt and pepper to taste

Step-by-Step Preparation:

1. Mix the shrimp, bell peppers, and baby corn in a microwave-safe dish.
2. In a separate bowl, combine soy sauce, oyster sauce, cornstarch, garlic, salt, and pepper to create the sauce.
3. Pour the sauce over the seafood and vegetables, mixing well to coat.
4. Microwave on high for about 8-10 minutes, stirring halfway through.
5. Let stand for a few minutes before serving.

Nutritional Facts: (Per serving)

- Calories: 150
- Protein: 20g
- Fat: 3g
- Carbohydrates: 10g
- Sodium: 800mg

Transform your kitchen into an Asian culinary adventure with this Chinese Seafood Medley of Shrimp. This quick, microwave-friendly dish offers a flavorful and healthy option for those who love exotic cuisine but need more time.

63: Fried Fish Fillet and Vegetables

Enjoy the rich flavors of the sea with this easy-to-make Fried Fish Fillet and Vegetable recipe. Perfect for a quick weeknight dinner, it's not just tasty but nutritious. Cooked in the microwave, it's all about convenience without compromising taste.

Servings: 4

Prepping Time: 15 Minutes

Cook Time: 15 Minutes

Difficulty: Easy

Ingredients:

- 4 Fish fillets (any white fish, deboned)
- 2 cups Mixed vegetables (carrots, beans, bell peppers)
- 2 tbsp Olive oil
- 2 cloves Garlic (minced)
- 1 tsp Lemon zest
- Salt and pepper to taste

Step-by-Step Preparation:

1. Season the fish fillets with salt, pepper, garlic, and lemon zest.
2. Place the fillets in a microwave-safe dish and drizzle with olive oil.
3. Microwave for 7 minutes, turning once.
4. Add mixed vegetables to the buzz around the fillets.
5. Microwave for another 7-8 minutes or until the vegetables are tender and the fish flakes easily.

Nutritional Facts: (Per serving)

- Calories: 285
- Protein: 35g
- Fat: 10g
- Carbohydrates: 15g
- Fiber: 4g

End your day on a delicious note with this Fried Fish Fillet and Vegetable recipe. It's as easy as it gets, proving that fast food can be healthy too. The fish's tenderness, the vegetables' crunchiness, and the lemon's zest will make your taste buds sing. Enjoy!

64: Spicy Cajun Shrimp With Rice

Discover the savory delight of this quick and easy Spicy Cajun Shrimp with Rice dish. Perfect for those who love a good kick of spice, this microwave-friendly recipe combines the vibrant flavors of the South with succulent shrimp, ready in just minutes.

Servings: 4

Prepping Time: 10 Minutes

Cook Time: 15 Minutes

Difficulty: Easy

Ingredients:

- 1 lb raw shrimp, peeled and deveined
- 2 cups of white rice
- 4 cups of water
- 1 tablespoon of Cajun spice
- 1 tablespoon of olive oil
- 2 cloves of garlic, minced
- Salt to taste
- Chopped parsley for garnish

Step-by-Step Preparation:

1. Combine rice and water in a microwave-safe dish, and cook on high for 10 minutes.
2. Mix shrimp, Cajun spice, olive oil, garlic, and salt in a separate bowl.
3. Spread the shrimp evenly on a microwave-safe dish, and cook on high for 5 minutes.
4. Once both are done, mix shrimp with rice, garnish with parsley, and serve hot.

Nutritional Facts: (Per serving)

- ❖ Calories: 350 kcal
- ❖ Protein: 24g
- ❖ Carbohydrates: 45g
- ❖ Fat: 8g
- ❖ Sodium: 120mg

The Spicy Cajun Shrimp with Rice recipe is easy and quick to make and packed with flavors. It's a beautiful way to bring a touch of the South to your kitchen table. This recipe makes eating a satisfying and flavorful meal more accessible than ever, even on the busiest days.

65: Seafood Gumbo

Savor the rich flavors of the bayou with this easy-to-prepare Seafood Gumbo. It's a convenient way to bring the taste of New Orleans into your home, even on a weeknight.

Servings: 4

Prepping Time: 15 minutes

Cook Time: 25 minutes

Difficulty: Easy

Ingredients:

- 1/2 cup butter
- 1/2 cup flour
- 1 cup chopped onion
- 1 cup chopped celery
- 1 cup chopped bell pepper
- 1 pound assorted seafood (shrimp, crab, oysters)
- 4 cups seafood stock
- 2 cups okra
- 2 cloves of garlic, minced

- ➢ Salt, pepper, and cayenne to taste
- ➢ 2 teaspoons gumbo file

Step-by-Step Preparation:

1. In a microwave-safe bowl, combine butter and flour. Microwave for 6 minutes, stirring every 2 minutes, until it becomes a roux.
2. Add onions, celery, bell pepper, and garlic to the roux and microwave for 5 minutes.
3. Stir in seafood stock, okra, seasonings, and seafood. Microwave for 14 minutes, stirring halfway through.
4. Stir in gumbo file, and let sit for 1 minute before serving.

Nutritional Facts: (Per serving)

- ❖ Calories: 465
- ❖ Protein: 32g
- ❖ Carbs: 23g
- ❖ Fat: 28g
- ❖ Sodium: 1045mg
- ❖ Fiber: 3g

Revel in the comforting, spicy warmth of homemade Seafood Gumbo. This microwave-friendly recipe gives you all the vibrant flavors of traditional gumbo without the fuss, allowing you to serve a soulful meal in just a few minutes. Enjoy!

66: Baja Fish Tacos With Mango Salsa

Embrace the vibrant flavors of the sea and tropical fruits with these delightful Baja Fish Tacos served with Mango Salsa. Easy to make, light, and packed with nutrients, it's perfect for a quick and satisfying meal.

Servings: 4

Prepping Time: 20 minutes

Cook Time: 5 minutes

Difficulty: Easy

Ingredients:

- 4 white fish fillets
- 1 tablespoon of olive oil
- Salt and pepper to taste
- 8 small corn tortillas
- 2 ripe mangoes
- 1 red onion
- 2 jalapenos
- 1 lime
- A handful of fresh cilantro

Step-by-Step Preparation:

1. Season fish fillets with olive oil, salt, and pepper. Microwave for 5 minutes.
2. While the fish cooks, dice mangoes, onion, jalapenos, and cilantro and combine in a bowl. Squeeze lime over the top and mix to create the salsa.
3. Warm tortillas in the microwave for about 30 seconds.
4. Flake the cooked fish and assemble your tacos by adding fish onto tortillas and topping with mango salsa.

Nutritional Facts: (Per serving)

- ❖ Calories: 325
- ❖ Protein: 28g
- ❖ Carbohydrates: 36g
- ❖ Dietary Fiber: 5g
- ❖ Fat: 8g

Discover the joy of coastal cuisine from your kitchen with these Baja Fish Tacos with Mango Salsa. Perfect for a simple weeknight dinner or craving something fresh and flavorful. A tremendous explosion of tastes that you can quickly put together, this recipe is sure to become a favorite in your household.

67: Chili Garlic Prawns Starter

Experience the incredible fusion of flavors with this easy, spicy, garlicky Chili Garlic Prawns Starter served with crispy bread. It's a microwave-friendly recipe, perfect for a quick appetizer or a light meal.

Servings: 4

Prepping Time: 15 minutes

Cook Time: 5 minutes

Difficulty: Easy

Ingredients:

- 500g prawns, peeled and deveined
- 4 cloves garlic, minced
- 2 tablespoons chili flakes
- 2 tablespoons olive oil
- Salt to taste
- 1 tablespoon lemon juice
- A handful of fresh parsley chopped
- 4 slices of bread

Step-by-Step Preparation:

1. Mix prawns, garlic, chili flakes, olive oil, and salt in a bowl.
2. Microwave the mixture for 4-5 minutes or until the prawns turn pink.
3. Stir in the lemon juice and sprinkle with fresh parsley.
4. Toast the bread slices until crispy.
5. Serve the prawns hot with the toasted bread.

Nutritional Facts: (Per serving)

- ❖ Calories: 250
- ❖ Protein: 24g
- ❖ Fat: 10g
- ❖ Carbohydrates: 16g
- ❖ Fiber: 1g

Indulge in this irresistible Chili Garlic Prawns Starter that is rich in flavors and incredibly quick to prepare. Its compelling blend of spices and garlic pairs perfectly with bread for a mouth-watering start to any meal. It's an effortless delight from your microwave to your table.

68: New England Clam Chowder

Delve into the world of seafood with this quick, easy-to-make, microwave-friendly version of the classic New England Clam Chowder, served with crispy crackers. Enjoy the richness of clams, creamy texture, and enticing flavors from your kitchen in no time.

Servings: 4

Prepping Time: 10 minutes

Cook Time: 15 minutes

Difficulty: Easy

Ingredients:

- 2 cans (6.5 oz each) of chopped clams in juice
- 1 cup diced potatoes
- 1/2 cup chopped onion
- 1/2 cup chopped celery
- 1 clove garlic, minced
- 2 cups milk
- 1 cup heavy cream
- 2 tablespoons unsalted butter

- ➢ Salt and pepper to taste
- ➢ Oyster crackers for serving

Step-by-Step Preparation:

1. Combine clams (with juice), potatoes, onion, celery, and garlic in a microwave-safe bowl. Microwave for 5 minutes.
2. Stir in milk, heavy cream, and butter. Microwave for another 10 minutes, stirring every 3 minutes.
3. Season with salt and pepper. Serve hot with oyster crackers on top.

Nutritional Facts: (Per serving)

- ❖ Calories: 370
- ❖ Protein: 16g
- ❖ Carbs: 24g
- ❖ Fat: 23g
- ❖ Sodium: 890mg

This hearty and comforting New England Clam Chowder brings the coastal flavors to your dinner table. Its simplicity and convenience make it a perfect dish for those cozy nights or a quick warm-up meal during the cooler months. Sit back and savor the richness of this classic chowder, cracker crunch, and all.

69: Portobello Mushroom Stuffed With Crab

Immerse yourself in a decadent seafood experience with this easy-to-make Portobello Mushroom Stuffed With Crab. A delightful fusion of hearty mushrooms and luxurious crab, this dish is perfect for weeknight dinners or sophisticated soirees.

Servings: 4

Prepping Time: 10 Minutes

Cook Time: 5 Minutes

Difficulty: Easy

Ingredients:

- 4 Portobello mushrooms
- 2 cups crab meat, drained
- 1/4 cup breadcrumbs
- 1/4 cup mayonnaise
- 1/4 cup grated Parmesan cheese
- 1 teaspoon lemon juice
- Salt and pepper to taste
- Fresh parsley for garnish

Step-by-Step Preparation:

1. Clean mushrooms and remove stems.
2. Mix crab, breadcrumbs, mayonnaise, cheese, lemon juice, salt, and pepper.
3. Stuff each mushroom with the crab mixture.
4. Place in a microwave-safe dish.
5. Cook on high in the microwave for 5 minutes.
6. Garnish with fresh parsley before serving.

Nutritional Facts: (Per serving)

- Calories: 225
- Protein: 20g
- Fat: 10g
- Carbs: 12g
- Fiber: 2g
- Sugar: 2g

Savor the luxury of a restaurant-quality seafood dish right at home with this Portobello Mushroom Stuffed With Crab. It's impressively flavorful, undeniably nourishing, and astoundingly easy to prepare - your go-to choice for a quick and delectable gourmet meal.

70: Seasoned Baked Lobster Tails

Start your gourmet journey with our easy and delectable Seasoned Baked Lobster Tails With Lemon recipe. This dish captures the luscious flavors of the sea, brightened with a zesty hint of lemon.

Servings: 4

Prepping Time: 20 minutes

Cook Time: 15 minutes

Difficulty: Easy

Ingredients:

- 4 lobster tails
- 4 tablespoons of butter
- 1 tablespoon of chopped parsley
- 1 garlic clove, minced
- 1 teaspoon of salt
- 1/2 teaspoon of black pepper
- 1 lemon, zested and juiced

Step-by-Step Preparation:

1. Rinse and pat dry the lobster tails.
2. Mix the butter, parsley, garlic, salt, pepper, and lemon zest.
3. Place lobster tails in a microwave-safe dish, and brush each with the seasoned butter mixture.
4. Microwave high for 12-15 minutes or until the lobster meat turns opaque.
5. Drizzle with fresh lemon juice before serving.

Nutritional Facts: (Per serving)

- Calories: 210
- Protein: 24g
- Carbohydrates: 2g
- Fat: 11g
- Sodium: 970mg
- Fiber: 0g

Bid farewell to bland seafood dinners and say hello to this radiant and savory dish. Our easy-to-make Seasoned Baked Lobster Tails With Lemon recipe is bound to impress your family and friends with its flavor-packed punch and simplicity.

Chapter 8: Sippable Delights Drinks & Smoothies

71: Hot Mulled Apple Cider

Indulge in fall's warm, comforting flavors with this Hot, Mulled Apple Cider recipe. This microwave-friendly recipe is perfect for a cozy night in, spiced with cinnamon sticks and bursting with the sweetness of apples.

Servings: 4

Prepping Time: 5 minutes

Cook Time: 5 minutes

Difficulty: Easy

Ingredients:

- 4 cups of apple cider
- 4 whole cinnamon sticks
- 8 whole cloves
- 1 orange, sliced
- 1 apple, sliced

Step-by-Step Preparation:

1. Combine all ingredients in a large microwave-safe bowl.
2. Microwave on high for 5 minutes or until hot.
3. Carefully strain the mixture into mugs, ensuring that spices and fruit slices are removed.
4. Serve hot with a cinnamon stick in each cup for added flavor.

Nutritional Facts: (Per serving)

- Calories: 130
- Protein: 0g
- Carbohydrates: 31g
- Fiber: 0g
- Fat: 0g
- Sugar: 24g

Experience the taste of autumn any time of the year with this easy and delightful Hot Mulled Apple Cider recipe. Perfect for gatherings or a quiet evening at home, it's a treat that warms the heart as much as it does the body.

72: Delicious Chocolate Stripped Croissants

Indulge in these delightful, homemade Chocolate Stripped Croissants. Perfect for a sweet breakfast treat or a gourmet dessert, this easy microwave recipe brings the bakery into your home and will impress your loved ones with its rich flavors and delicious look.

Servings: 6

Prepping Time: 15 Minutes

Cook Time: 2 Minutes

Difficulty: Easy

Ingredients:

- 1 Can Refrigerated Croissant Dough
- 1/2 Cup Dark Chocolate Chips
- 1 Egg (for egg wash)
- 1 Tbsp Powdered Sugar (for dusting)

Step-by-Step Preparation:

1. Roll out your croissant dough and cut it into triangles.

2. Place a small amount of chocolate chips in the broader end of each triangle.
3. Roll the dough towards the narrower end, encapsulating the chocolate chips.
4. Brush each croissant with egg wash for a golden finish.
5. Microwave for 2 minutes or until they puff up and become golden.
6. Let cool for a few minutes, then dust with powdered sugar.

Nutritional Facts: (Per serving)

- Calories: 210 kcal
- Protein: 3g
- Carbohydrates: 24g
- Fat: 12g
- Sugar: 7g

Delight your senses with these easy and quick Chocolate Stripped Croissants, made right in your microwave. Whether you seek a decadent start to your day or a luscious dessert after dinner, these croissants will meet your desires while filling your kitchen with a delicious aroma. Enjoy baking and savor the compliments!

73: Healthy Ginger Tea With Lemon

Embrace the soothing power of healthy ginger tea with lemon, a comforting brew full of aromatic zest and natural health benefits. This refreshing tea can be made easily in the microwave, perfect for a cozy evening or a refreshing morning start.

Servings: 2

Prepping Time: 5 minutes

Cook Time: 2 minutes

Difficulty: Easy

Ingredients:

- 2 cups water
- 1 inch fresh ginger, thinly sliced
- 1 lemon
- 2 teaspoons honey, optional

Step-by-Step Preparation:

1. Pour water into a microwave-safe container and add ginger slices.
2. Microwave for 2 minutes.

3. Carefully remove from the microwave and add the juice of one lemon.
4. Stir in honey if desired.
5. Strain into cups and serve hot.

Nutritional Facts: (Per serving)

- Calories: 30
- Fat: 0g
- Carbohydrates: 8g
- Fiber: 1g
- Protein: 0g

This simple yet healthy ginger tea with lemon is a recipe for rejuvenation. The bright, zingy lemon blends with the warm. Spicy ginger for a taste that is both healing and pleasing. Not just a delightful beverage, this tea is a natural remedy to brighten your day.

74: Vegan Almond & Coconut Chocolate Smoothie

Imagine a delightful and healthy experience with our Vegan Almond & Coconut Chocolate Smoothie. This recipe combines the creamy texture of almond and coconut milk with the rich taste of cocoa. With just a few ingredients and your microwave, this smoothie is perfect for a quick breakfast or an indulgent dessert.

Servings: 2

Prepping Time: 10 minutes

Cook Time: 2 minutes

Difficulty: Easy

Ingredients:

- 1 cup Unsweetened Almond Milk
- 1 cup Coconut Milk
- 2 tablespoons Unsweetened Cocoa Powder
- 2 tablespoons Maple Syrup
- 1/2 cup Vegan Dark Chocolate Chips
- 1 teaspoon Vanilla Extract

Step-by-Step Preparation:

1. Combine almond milk, coconut milk, cocoa powder, and maple syrup in a blender and blend until smooth.
2. Pour the mixture into a microwave-safe bowl and add vegan dark chocolate chips.
3. Microwave for 2 minutes or until the chocolate chips are fully melted. Stir well to combine.
4. Add vanilla extract and give it a final stir.
5. Pour the smoothie into glasses and serve immediately.

Nutritional Facts: (Per serving)

- Calories: 280 kcal
- Protein: 4g
- Carbohydrates: 22g
- Fiber: 3g
- Fat: 20g

This Vegan Almond & Coconut Chocolate Smoothie is more than just a satisfying treat; it's a nutrient-packed powerhouse! It's perfect for any time of day with an appealing blend of rich chocolate flavor and creamy texture. So, why wait? Indulge in this deliciously accessible, microwave-friendly recipe and bring a touch of sweet luxury to your daily routine.

75: Pumpkin Spice Late With Cinnamon

Savor the comforting tastes of autumn with this homemade Pumpkin Spice Latte with Cinnamon. A delightful blend of aromatic spices, coffee, and milk that's easily prepared in your microwave. Now you can enjoy a cafe-style treat anytime at home.

Servings: 2

Prepping Time: 5 minutes

Cook Time: 2 minutes

Difficulty: Easy

Ingredients:

- 2 cups of milk
- 2 tablespoons of pumpkin puree
- 1 to 3 tablespoons of sugar (to taste)
- 1 tablespoon of vanilla extract
- 1/2 teaspoon of pumpkin spice
- 1/2 cup of strong hot coffee
- Whipped cream and cinnamon (for topping)

Step-by-Step Preparation:

1. Whisk together milk, pumpkin puree, sugar, and spices in a microwave-safe bowl.
2. Microwave the mixture on high for 1-2 minutes until hot.
3. Stir in the hot coffee and vanilla extract.
4. Pour the mixture into two mugs, then top with whipped cream and a sprinkle of cinnamon.

Nutritional Facts: (Per serving)

- Calories: 190
- Protein: 8g
- Carbohydrates: 25g
- Fat: 6g
- Sodium: 120mg
- Fiber: 1g

Indulge in the season's warmth with this easy and delightful Pumpkin Spice Latte with Cinnamon. It's the perfect way to start a crisp autumn morning or unwind after a long day. Enjoy this cafe-style luxury from the comfort of your own home.

76: Milk Shakes With Blackberries

Immerse yourself in the delectable pleasure of Tasty Fresh Milk Shakes with Blackberries. This refreshing drink is a delightful concoction of creamy milk and juicy blackberries, a perfect refreshment for any day or night.

Servings: 4

Prepping Time: 10 minutes

Cook Time: 0 minutes

Difficulty: Easy

Ingredients:

- 2 cups of fresh blackberries
- 4 cups of chilled milk
- 4 tablespoons of sugar
- 1 teaspoon of vanilla extract
- Crushed ice (optional)

Step-by-Step Preparation:

1. Rinse the fresh blackberries thoroughly and pat them dry.

2. Combine the blackberries, milk, sugar, and vanilla extract in a blender.
3. Blend until smooth.
4. If desired, add crushed ice for an extra chill factor.
5. Pour the shake into glasses and serve immediately.

Nutritional Facts: (Per serving)

- Calories: 220 kcal
- Carbohydrates: 26g
- Protein: 8g
- Fat: 10g
- Saturated Fat: 6g
- Sodium: 125mg
- Fiber: 3g
- Sugar: 20g

End your day with a burst of flavor from these Tasty Fresh Milk Shakes with Blackberries. Not only are they delicious, but they're also an excellent source of essential nutrients and antioxidants. So, indulge your taste buds while keeping your health in check!

77: Pineapple Smoothie

Kick-start your day with a refreshing Pineapple Smoothie! This easy-to-make microwave dish is an excellent blend of sweet and tangy flavors, making it a perfect drink for hot summer days or as a nutritious post-workout snack.

Servings: 2

Prepping Time: 10 minutes

Cook Time: 2 minutes

Difficulty: Easy

Ingredients:

- 2 cups fresh pineapple, chopped
- 1 ripe banana
- 1 cup unsweetened almond milk
- 1 tablespoon honey
- Ice cubes

Step-by-Step Preparation:

1. Place the chopped pineapple, banana, almond milk, and honey in a blender.

2. Blend until smooth.
3. Pour the smoothie into microwave-safe glasses.
4. Microwave on high for 2 minutes or until warmed to your liking.
5. Stir in ice cubes before serving.

Nutritional Facts: (Per serving)

- ❖ Calories: 180
- ❖ Protein: 2g
- ❖ Carbohydrates: 40g
- ❖ Fat: 3g
- ❖ Fiber: 3g
- ❖ Sugar: 29g

Whip up this Pineapple Smoothie in minutes and embrace the tropical vibes! It's a delicious, healthy, and refreshing way to get your daily dose of vitamins and minerals, making it a fantastic addition to your morning routine or post-workout recovery. Enjoy!

78: Strawberry Banana Smoothie Bowl

Kickstart your day with this vibrant Strawberry Banana Smoothie Bowl. Easy to prepare, it's an excellent choice for a healthy, wholesome breakfast or a quick afternoon snack. Loaded with fresh fruits and topped with granola and chia seeds, it's a great way to add some zest to your routine.

Servings: 2

Prepping Time: 10 minutes

Cook Time: 0 minutes

Difficulty: Easy

Ingredients:

- 1 banana
- 1 cup fresh strawberries
- 1/2 cup almond milk
- 1 tablespoon honey
- 2 tablespoons granola
- 1 tablespoon chia seeds
- Fresh fruits for topping

Step-by-Step Preparation:

1. Blend the banana, strawberries, almond milk, and honey until smooth.
2. Pour the mixture into two bowls.
3. Top each bowl with granola, chia seeds, and your choice of fresh fruits.
4. Serve immediately and enjoy!

Nutritional Facts: (Per serving)

- Calories: 220
- Protein: 6g
- Carbohydrates: 40g
- Fat: 5g
- Fiber: 7g
- Sugar: 22g

Transform your regular breakfast into an exciting feast with this Strawberry Banana Smoothie Bowl. Not only is it packed with nutrients, but it's also visually appealing, making your mornings or snack times even more enjoyable. It's a delicious, healthy alternative that everyone in the family will love.

79: A Hearty and Healthy Oatmeal

Start your day right with a warm bowl of hearty and healthy oatmeal. This easy-to-make microwave recipe ensures a nutritious breakfast in minutes, saving time and energizing you throughout the day.

Servings: 2

Prepping Time: 5 minutes

Cook Time: 2 minutes

Difficulty: Easy

Ingredients:

- 1 cup of oats
- 2 cups of water or milk
- 1-2 tablespoons of honey or maple syrup
- Fresh fruits and nuts for topping (optional)

Step-by-Step Preparation:

1. Combine oats and water or milk in a microwave-safe bowl.
2. Microwave on high for 2 minutes.

3. Carefully remove the bowl (it will be hot), and stir in the sweetener.
4. Top with fresh fruits and nuts if desired.
5. Serve hot.

Nutritional Facts: (Per serving)

- Calories: 155
- Protein: 6g
- Carbs: 27g
- Fiber: 4g
- Sugar: 6g
- Fat: 3g

Revitalize your mornings with this healthy and hearty oatmeal dish. Quick to prepare, this versatile dish allows you to add your favorite fruits and nuts for extra flavor and nutrition. A serving of this oatmeal ensures a good start, providing substantial energy to power your day.

80: Tea With Milk or Chai Latte

Take the plunge into comforting beverages with this easy homemade milk tea, a Chai Latte. It's a perfect blend of robust black tea, creamy milk, and aromatic spices, ready in just minutes using a microwave!

Servings: 2

Prepping Time: 5 minutes

Cook Time: 2 minutes

Difficulty: Easy

Ingredients:

- 2 cups of milk
- 2 black tea bags
- 1 tablespoon sugar (or to taste)
- 1/2 teaspoon ground cinnamon
- 1/4 teaspoon ground cardamom
- 1/4 teaspoon ground ginger

Step-by-Step Preparation:

1. In a microwave-safe bowl, combine milk, sugar, and spices. Stir until mixed.
2. Heat the mixture in the microwave for 1 minute.
3. Add the tea bags and microwave for another minute.
4. Let the tea steep for about 3 minutes, then remove the tea bags.
5. Stir well and serve hot.

Nutritional Facts: (Per serving)

- Calories: 150
- Protein: 8g
- Carbs: 12g
- Fat: 8g
- Sugar: 10g

Indulge in this simple yet divine homemade milk tea anytime you need a cozy beverage. This Chai Latte is not only a stress-buster but also a fantastic way to brighten your morning or wind down your evening. Enjoy this easy microwave recipe to warm your soul!

Chapter 9: Super Speedy Super Fresh Salads

81: Warm Autumn Quinoa Salad

This warm autumn quinoa salad blends the heartiness of quinoa with the comforting flavors of baked sweet potatoes and Brussels sprouts. It's an easy yet vibrant microwave recipe perfect for a quick lunch or dinner in the chillier months.

Servings: 4

Prepping Time: 15 minutes

Cook Time: 20 minutes

Difficulty: Easy

Ingredients:

- 1 cup quinoa
- 2 cups vegetable broth
- 2 sweet potatoes, cubed
- 2 cups Brussels sprouts, halved
- 1 tablespoon olive oil

- Salt and pepper to taste
- 1/4 cup dried cranberries
- 1/4 cup chopped pecans

Step-by-Step Preparation:

1. Rinse quinoa and cook in the microwave with vegetable broth for 15 minutes.
2. While cooking quinoa, toss sweet potatoes and Brussels sprouts in olive oil, salt, and pepper. Bake in the microwave for 10 minutes.
3. Mix cooked quinoa, baked vegetables, dried cranberries, and pecans.
4. Serve warm; season to taste if needed.

Nutritional Facts: (Per serving)

- Calories: 300
- Protein: 8g
- Carbs: 55g
- Fiber: 8g
- Fat: 7g

Packed with nutrition and bursting with flavor, this warm autumn quinoa salad makes healthy eating effortless. In just 35 minutes, you have a comforting dish perfect for a cozy autumn night. Try this easy recipe and elevate your weeknight dinner game.

82: Salad With Shrimps

Introduce a burst of flavor to your meal with this stunning Salad with Shrimp, Avocado, Tomatoes, Onions, and Seeds. It's a wonderfully balanced dish combining sweet, sour, and savory flavors with different textures, perfect for a quick lunch or a hearty dinner.

Servings: 4

Prepping Time: 15 minutes

Cook Time: 2 minutes

Difficulty: Easy

Ingredients:

- 1 lb. peeled shrimp
- 2 ripe avocados, diced
- 2 cups cherry tomatoes, halved
- 1 red onion, thinly sliced
- 4 tablespoons mixed seeds (sunflower, pumpkin)
- Juice of 1 lemon
- Olive oil, salt, and pepper

Step-by-Step Preparation:

1. Rinse the shrimp and pat dry. Place in a microwave-safe bowl, drizzle with olive oil, and season with salt and pepper—microwave for 2 minutes or until shrimps turn pink.
2. Combine the cooked shrimp, avocados, cherry tomatoes, onions, and seeds in a large bowl.
3. Drizzle with lemon juice and a bit more olive oil—season with salt and pepper to taste. Toss gently to combine.

Nutritional Facts: (Per serving)

- ❖ Calories: 350 kcal
- ❖ Protein: 24 g
- ❖ Fat: 21 g
- ❖ Carbohydrates: 20 g
- ❖ Fiber: 7 g
- ❖ Sodium: 460 mg

Savor the invigorating freshness of this easy-to-make salad featuring shrimp, avocado, tomatoes, onions, and seeds. It's not just about the enticing combination of tastes but also the nutritional benefits that make this dish a delightful addition to your everyday menu. Enjoy this salad as is, or add your favorite dressing to elevate its flavor profile.

83: Chickpea Salad With Tomatoes

Embrace the vibrant flavors of summer with this refreshing Chickpea Salad with Tomatoes. This light yet hearty salad combines nutrient-dense chickpeas, juicy tomatoes, and a blend of herbs, perfect for a quick lunch or an effortless side dish.

Servings: 4

Prepping Time: 10 minutes

Cook Time: 2 minutes

Difficulty: Easy

Ingredients:

- 2 cans (15 ounces each) of chickpeas, drained and rinsed
- 1 cup cherry tomatoes, halved
- 1 small red onion, finely chopped
- 1/4 cup fresh parsley, chopped
- 2 tablespoons olive oil
- Juice of 1 lemon
- Salt and pepper to taste

Step-by-Step Preparation:

1. Combine chickpeas, cherry tomatoes, red onion, and parsley in a large bowl.
2. Whisk together olive oil, lemon juice, salt, and pepper in a separate bowl.
3. Pour the dressing over the chickpea mixture and stir until well combined.
4. Microwave the salad for 2 minutes until slightly warmed. Stir before serving.

Nutritional Facts: (Per serving)

- Calories: 290
- Protein: 10g
- Carbohydrates: 40g
- Fat: 10g
- Fiber: 10g
- Sugar: 5g

Redefine your summer fare with this Chickpea Salad with Tomatoes - a fulfilling and nourishing meal ready in no time. This easy-to-make recipe brings out the best natural flavors, making it the perfect addition to your health-conscious culinary repertoire.

84: Teriyaki Chicken With Salad

Savor the taste of Asian cuisine from home with this easy Teriyaki Chicken with Salad and Rice recipe. No need for takeout when you can enjoy this delicious, nutritious. And microwave-friendly meal in minutes, perfect for busy weeknights.

Servings: 4

Prepping Time: 10 minutes

Cook Time: 15 minutes

Difficulty: Easy

Ingredients:

- 4 chicken breasts
- 1 cup teriyaki sauce
- 1 cup jasmine rice
- 2 cups water
- 1 head of lettuce
- 1 cucumber
- 2 carrots
- Sesame seeds for garnish

Step-by-Step Preparation:

1. Place the chicken in a microwave-safe dish, pour over the teriyaki sauce, cover, and microwave for 10-12 minutes or until cooked through.
2. While the chicken is cooking, rinse the rice and put it in a microwave-safe bowl with water. Cook for 10-12 minutes or until tender.
3. Prepare the salad by chopping the lettuce, cucumber, and carrots.
4. Once everything is ready, assemble the dish by slicing the chicken, serving it with rice, and the salad on the side. Sprinkle sesame seeds for garnish.

Nutritional Facts: (Per serving)

- Calories: 450
- Protein: 35g
- Carbohydrates: 50g
- Fiber: 4g
- Fat: 10g
- Sodium: 1400mg

Enjoy your homemade Teriyaki Chicken with Salad and Rice, which combines savory, sweet, and refreshing flavors. As a bonus, it's filled with wholesome ingredients that are good for you. Eating well has never been this simple or delicious!

85: Southwest Black Bean Lime Salad

This Southwest Black Bean Lime Salad introduces a burst of flavor and freshness to your mealtime. A simple, healthy, and colorful dish that combines various nutritious ingredients makes the perfect side of a light lunch.

Servings: 4

Prepping Time: 10 minutes

Cook Time: 2 minutes

Difficulty: Easy

Ingredients:

- 2 cans of black beans, rinsed and drained
- 1 red bell pepper, diced
- 1 green bell pepper, diced
- 1 cup corn kernels
- 1 medium red onion, diced
- Juice of 2 limes
- 2 tablespoons of olive oil
- 1/2 cup fresh cilantro, chopped

> Salt and pepper to taste

Step-by-Step Preparation:

1. Combine black beans, bell peppers, corn, and red onion in a large bowl.
2. Whisk together lime juice, olive oil, salt, and pepper in a separate bowl.
3. Pour the dressing over the salad and toss until well combined.
4. Stir in the chopped cilantro.
5. Microwave the salad for 2 minutes to melt the flavors together.
6. Serve immediately or refrigerate for later use.

Nutritional Facts: (Per serving)

- Calories: 240
- Protein: 9g
- Fat: 7g
- Carbohydrates: 37g
- Fiber: 10g
- Sodium: 340mg

This Southwest Black Bean Lime Salad combines the southwest's vibrant flavors in a quick and easy microwave dish. Packed with protein, fiber, and a wealth of vitamins, it's an ideal recipe for those seeking a healthy yet utterly delicious culinary experience.

86: Cobb Salad

Savor the mouthwatering delight of the classic Cobb Salad, now conveniently designed for your microwave! This simplified take on the timeless American dish captures its wholesome ingredients and rich flavors, ideal for a healthy and hearty lunch or dinner.

Servings: 2

Prepping Time: 15 minutes

Cook Time: 2 minutes

Difficulty: Easy

Ingredients:

- 2 cups mixed salad greens
- 1 chicken breast, cooked and diced
- 1 hard-boiled egg, sliced
- 1 avocado, diced
- 1 small tomato, diced
- 2 strips of bacon, cooked and crumbled
- 1/4 cup blue cheese crumbles
- Ranch dressing to taste

Step-by-Step Preparation:

1. Arrange the salad greens in a microwave-safe dish.
2. Evenly distribute chicken, egg, avocado, tomato, bacon, and blue cheese over the gardens.
3. Cover the dish and microwave on high for 2 minutes to slightly warm the ingredients.
4. Drizzle with ranch dressing and serve immediately.

Nutritional Facts: (Per serving)

- ❖ Calories: 375 kcal
- ❖ Protein: 28 g
- ❖ Carbohydrates: 12 g
- ❖ Fat: 25 g
- ❖ Saturated Fat: 7 g
- ❖ Fiber: 6 g
- ❖ Sugar: 3 g

Relish the refreshing, healthful combination of the Microwave Cobb Salad. Its fusion of proteins, vegetables, and flavorsome dressing offers a delicious, quick, and nutritious meal that's perfect for the busy gourmet on the go. Delight in the simplicity of cooking and the complexity of flavors right from your microwave!

87: Pasta Salad With Grilled Vegetables

Indulge in a delicious fusion of Italian and summer flavors with this Pasta Salad with Grilled Vegetables recipe. This easy-to-make microwave dish combines the wholesomeness of vegetables and pasta, creating a perfect meal for any time of the day.

Servings: 4

Prepping Time: 15 minutes

Cook Time: 15 minutes

Difficulty: Easy

Ingredients:

- 2 cups of pasta
- 1 cup of bell peppers, assorted colors
- 1 cup of zucchini
- 1/2 cup of red onion
- 2 tablespoons of olive oil
- Salt and pepper to taste
- 1/2 cup of Italian dressing
- 1/4 cup of grated Parmesan cheese

Step-by-Step Preparation:

1. Microwave pasta according to the package instructions, then drain and let it cool.
2. Slice and coat the vegetables with olive oil, salt, and pepper. Microwave-grill them for 5-7 minutes until tender.
3. In a large bowl, mix the cooled pasta and grilled vegetables.
4. Add Italian dressing and grated Parmesan cheese to the bowl, then toss until everything is well coated.

Nutritional Facts: (Per serving)

- Calories: 320
- Protein: 10g
- Carbs: 44g
- Fat: 12g
- Fiber: 3g

Pasta Salad with Grilled Vegetables is ideal for a quick, nutritious meal or entertaining guests on summer nights. It is easy to prepare in a microwave and adds an Italian twist to your regular salad, ensuring you enjoy a vibrant, healthy, and delightful dining experience.

88: Italian Chopped Salad

Experience the freshness of Italy in your own home with this Italian Chopped Salad. Vibrant, healthy, and bursting with flavors, it's a perfect side dish or light meal for those on the go. Enjoy the ease of this microwave-friendly recipe.

Servings: 4

Prepping Time: 15 minutes

Cook Time: 0 minutes

Difficulty: Easy

Ingredients:

- 2 cups romaine lettuce, chopped
- 1 cup cherry tomatoes, halved
- 1 cup cucumber, diced
- 1/2 cup red onion, thinly sliced
- 1/2 cup black olives, sliced
- 1/2 cup mozzarella cheese, cubed
- 1/2 cup salami, diced
- 1/4 cup olive oil

- ➢ 2 tbsp red wine vinegar
- ➢ Salt and pepper to taste

Step-by-Step Preparation:

1. In a large bowl, combine lettuce, tomatoes, cucumber, onion, olives, cheese, and salami.
2. Whisk together olive oil, red wine vinegar, salt, and pepper in a separate bowl.
3. Drizzle the dressing over the salad and toss to combine well.
4. Divide the salad among four plates and serve immediately.

Nutritional Facts: (Per serving)

- ❖ Calories: 240
- ❖ Fat: 18g
- ❖ Protein: 9g
- ❖ Carbohydrates: 8g
- ❖ Fiber: 2g
- ❖ Sugar: 4g
- ❖ Sodium: 800mg

Enjoy this Italian Chopped Salad as a standalone meal or a vibrant accompaniment to your main course. Quick to prepare and without cooking, this easy, microwave-friendly dish offers a delicious way to eat healthy wherever you are.

89: Blueberries Cranberry Salad

Add some fresh color to your table with this Blueberry Cranberry Salad. This simple microwave dish bursts with flavors, combining sweet blueberries, tangy cranberries, and crunchy almonds. It's a refreshing addition to any meal that can easily be prepared in under 10 minutes.

Servings: 4

Prepping Time: 5 minutes

Cook Time: 2 minutes

Difficulty: Easy

Ingredients:

- 2 cups fresh blueberries
- 1 cup dried cranberries
- 1/2 cup sliced almonds
- 2 tablespoons honey
- 1 tablespoon fresh lemon juice

Step-by-Step Preparation:

1. Mix blueberries, cranberries, and almonds in a microwave-safe bowl.
2. In a separate bowl, whisk together honey and lemon juice.
3. Drizzle the honey mixture over the fruit and almonds, stirring to combine.
4. Microwave the salad for 2 minutes, until warm.
5. Serve immediately.

Nutritional Facts: (Per serving)

- Calories: 180
- Protein: 3g
- Carbohydrates: 36g
- Fiber: 4g
- Fat: 4g
- Sugar: 28g

Indulge in this delightful blend of fruity flavors with the Blueberry Cranberry Salad. It's easy to whip up and incredibly healthy, with its nutrient-packed fruits and heart-friendly almonds the perfect side or dessert. To brighten your day, whether dining alone or hosting a feast.

90: Healthy Grilled Chicken Caesar Salad

Savor the delight of a healthy Caesar salad reinvented with juicy grilled chicken. This easy-to-make dish brings the restaurant experience to your dining table, providing a wholesome and nutritious meal combining fresh veggies and high-quality protein.

> **Servings:** 4
>
> **Prepping Time:** 15 minutes
>
> **Cook Time:** 15 minutes
>
> **Difficulty:** Easy

Ingredients:

> - 2 boneless, skinless chicken breasts
> - 1 tablespoon olive oil
> - Salt and pepper to taste
> - 2 romaine lettuce heads, washed and chopped
> - 1/2 cup Caesar salad dressing
> - 1/4 cup grated Parmesan cheese
> - 1 cup whole-grain croutons

Step-by-Step Preparation:

1. Rub the chicken breasts with olive oil, salt, and pepper.
2. Grill the chicken in a microwave for 10 minutes until fully cooked.
3. Allow the chicken to cool slightly before slicing into thin strips.
4. Combine the lettuce, Caesar dressing, and Parmesan cheese in a large bowl.
5. Add the grilled chicken and croutons, tossing gently to combine.
6. Serve immediately, with additional cheese on top if desired.

Nutritional Facts: (Per serving)

- Calories: 350 kcal
- Protein: 30 g
- Fat: 16 g
- Carbohydrates: 20 g
- Fiber: 3 g
- Sodium: 750 mg

Immerse yourself in the guilt-free indulgence of this Healthy Grilled Chicken Caesar Salad. Easy to prepare in a microwave, this dish brings a perfect balance of crunch and flavor, making your meal times memorable. It's a delightful blend of nutrition and taste, providing a robust punch to your regular salad routine.

Chapter 10: Decadent Desserts in a Snap

91: Chocolate Lava Cake Dusted

This quick and easy Chocolate Lava Cake Dusted recipe introduces the sweet magic of molten delight in your everyday dessert. Ideal for surprise guests, kids' parties, or when your sweet tooth craves a midnight snack. Experience a delicious journey of a perfectly cooked outer shell encasing a gooey chocolatey center.

Servings: 4

Prepping Time: 10 minutes

Cook Time: 1.5 minutes

Difficulty: Easy

Ingredients:

- 4 squares of semi-sweet baking chocolate
- 1/2 cup of unsalted butter
- 1 cup of powdered sugar
- 2 eggs

- ➢ 2 egg yolks
- ➢ 6 tablespoons of all-purpose flour
- ➢ Powdered sugar for dusting

Step-by-Step Preparation:

1. In a microwave-safe bowl, melt chocolate and butter, stirring every 30 seconds.
2. Whisk in powdered sugar until well blended.
3. Add eggs and egg yolks and stir until incorporated.
4. Stir in flour. Divide the mixture between 4 microwave-safe ramekins.
5. Microwave each ramekin for 1 minute 30 seconds or until the sides are firm and the center is soft.
6. Let it stand for 1 minute. Carefully run a knife around the cakes to loosen them. Invert onto dessert dishes. Dust with powdered sugar and serve immediately.

Nutritional Facts: (Per serving)

- ❖ Calories: 300
- ❖ Fat: 22g
- ❖ Carbohydrates: 24g
- ❖ Protein: 5g
- ❖ Fiber: 1g
- ❖ Sugar: 19g

Savor the burst of chocolate in every spoon of this chocolate lava cake dusted, a recipe as easy as pie and twice as delicious! Not only will this make your day, but it will also leave you with a lingering, rich aftertaste, reminding you of the delightful dessert journey you embarked upon. Enjoy this microwave miracle when the chocolate craving strikes next!

92: Creamy Rice Kheer (Khir)

Experience the luxurious, traditional taste of Indian cuisine in your own home with this easy microwave recipe for Creamy Rice Kheer. This heavenly dessert infuses fragrant spices into creamy rice for an unforgettable delightful treat.

Servings: 4

Prepping Time: 10 minutes

Cook Time: 20 minutes

Difficulty: Easy

Ingredients:

- 1/2 cup Basmati rice
- 4 cups whole milk
- 1/2 cup sugar
- 1/4 cup chopped nuts (cashews or almonds)
- 1/2 teaspoon cardamom powder
- A pinch of saffron strands

Step-by-Step Preparation:

1. Rinse the Basmati rice under cold water until the water clears, then drain.
2. Combine the rice and milk in a microwave-safe bowl.
3. Microwave the mixture for 10 minutes, stirring every 2-3 minutes.
4. Add the sugar, nuts, cardamom, and saffron. Stir well.
5. Microwave for another 10 minutes or until the rice is soft and the milk is creamy.
6. Let the Kheer cool before serving; it will thicken as it cools.

Nutritional Facts: (Per serving)

- Calories: 280
- Protein: 8g
- Carbohydrates: 45g
- Fat: 9g
- Cholesterol: 20mg
- Sodium: 105mg

Enjoy this Creamy Rice Kheer, a heavenly dessert that whisks you away to the colorful streets of India. It's simple to make and rich in flavors, making it the perfect ending to your family meal or a festive feast. A dessert so delightful, it will surely leave you wanting more.

93: Mug Cakes With Berries

Dive into a world of quick delights with these Mug Cakes With Berries, an easy microwave recipe. Get ready to whip up a delightful dessert with juicy berries that will bring sweetness to your palate in minutes.

Servings: 2

Prepping Time: 5 minutes

Cook Time: 2 minutes

Difficulty: Easy

Ingredients:

- 4 tablespoons all-purpose flour
- 2 tablespoons granulated sugar
- 1/4 teaspoon baking powder
- 3 tablespoons milk
- 2 tablespoons vegetable oil
- 1/2 teaspoon vanilla extract
- 2 tablespoons mixed berries

Step-by-Step Preparation:

1. In a microwave-safe mug, combine flour, sugar, and baking powder.
2. Stir in the milk, oil, and vanilla extract until smooth.
3. Add the mixed berries on top.
4. Microwave on high for 1.5-2 minutes until risen.
5. Let cool for a few minutes before serving.

Nutritional Facts: (Per serving)

- Calories: 265
- Protein: 3g
- Carbs: 25g
- Fat: 16g
- Fiber: 1g
- Sugar: 13g

Indulge in the sweet simplicity of Mug Cakes With Berries, a dessert you can prepare in the blink of an eye. It is the perfect solution for your late-night cravings and adds a dose of delightful berries to keep things fresh and flavorful.

94: Cinnabon Cake in Mug

Indulge in the sweetness of a Cinnabon in a mug with this simple and quick recipe! Treat your taste buds with a comforting dessert, blending the rich flavors of cinnamon, sugar, and cream cheese. It's perfect for a late-night craving or a leisurely morning treat!

Servings: 2

Prepping Time: 5 minutes

Cook Time: 2 minutes

Difficulty: Easy

Ingredients:

- 4 tablespoons all-purpose flour
- 2 tablespoons granulated sugar
- 1/4 teaspoon baking powder
- 3 tablespoons milk
- 2 tablespoons vegetable oil
- 1/4 teaspoon vanilla extract
- 1/2 teaspoon cinnamon

For Cream Cheese Frosting:

- ✓ 2 tablespoons cream cheese
- ✓ 1 tablespoon powdered sugar

Step-by-Step Preparation:

1. Combine flour, sugar, baking powder, and cinnamon in a microwave-safe mug.
2. Stir in milk, oil, and vanilla extract until smooth.
3. Microwave the cup for about 2 minutes.
4. Meanwhile, mix cream cheese and powdered sugar to prepare the frosting.
5. Once the cake is made, let it cool briefly before topping it with the frosting.

Nutritional Facts: (Per serving)

- ❖ Calories: 280
- ❖ Protein: 3.5g
- ❖ Carbohydrates: 35g
- ❖ Fat: 14g
- ❖ Sodium: 130mg

With this Cinnabon Cake in a Mug, it's easy to enjoy a warm, delicious treat without leaving the comfort of your home. This recipe provides a balance of sweetness, creaminess, and a touch of cinnamon spice that's perfect for any time of the day. Get your mug ready and savor every bite!

95: Apple Crisp With Whipped Cream

Introduce the joy of baking into your kitchen without the fuss. Our Apple Crisp with Whipped Cream offers a delightful medley of tart apples, cinnamon sweetness, and a crispy crumble, all topped with a dollop of smooth whipped cream. This a simple yet delicious microwave recipe everyone will love.

> **Servings:** 4
>
> **Prepping Time:** 15 minutes
>
> **Cook Time:** 10 minutes
>
> **Difficulty:** Easy

Ingredients:

- 4 medium-sized apples, peeled and chopped
- 1 cup of oatmeal
- 1/2 cup of brown sugar
- 1/4 cup of all-purpose flour
- 1/2 tsp of cinnamon
- 1/4 cup of unsalted butter, melted
- 1 cup of whipped cream

Step-by-Step Preparation:

1. In a microwave-safe dish, layer the chopped apples evenly.
2. Mix the oatmeal, brown sugar, flour, and cinnamon in a separate bowl. Add the melted butter and mix until it forms crumbles.
3. Sprinkle this mixture over the apples.
4. Microwave on high for 10 minutes or until the top turns golden brown.
5. Let it cool slightly, then serve with a dollop of whipped cream.

Nutritional Facts: (Per serving)

- Calories: 365
- Protein: 3g
- Carbohydrates: 60g
- Fat: 15g
- Fiber: 6g
- Sugar: 40g

Now, savor the taste of this homemade Apple Crisp with Whipped Cream. It's a sweet, crisp, and creamy treat for any occasion. Enjoy a restaurant-style dessert at home with the convenience of a microwave and minimal prep time. This dish promises satisfaction for your sweet tooth with an irresistible simplicity.

96: Chocolate Chip Cookies

Indulge in a quick sweet treat with these easy microwave Light Chocolate Chip Cookies. With just a handful of ingredients and a microwave, your cookie cravings will be satisfied in minutes. The recipe yields three delightful cookies, perfect for a snack or dessert.

Servings: 1

Prepping Time: 5 minutes

Cook Time: 2 minutes

Difficulty: Easy

Ingredients:

- 1 tablespoon butter
- 1 tablespoon white sugar
- 1 tablespoon brown sugar
- 1/8 teaspoon vanilla extract
- 1/4 cup all-purpose flour
- 1/8 teaspoon baking soda
- Pinch of salt
- 2 tablespoons chocolate chips

Step-by-Step Preparation:

1. In a microwave-safe bowl, melt the butter.
2. Stir in the sugars and vanilla extract until smooth.
3. Mix in the flour, baking soda, and salt.
4. Fold in the chocolate chips.
5. Divide the cookie dough into three portions.
6. Place each piece on a microwave-safe plate and flatten slightly.
7. Microwave each cookie for about 30-40 seconds or until golden brown.
8. Let them cool for a minute before enjoying them.

Nutritional Facts: (Per serving)

- Calories: 280
- Fat: 14g
- Carbs: 35g
- Protein: 3g

Feeling spontaneous or need a fast dessert? These easy, microwave-friendly, Light Chocolate Chip Cookies are your perfect solution. You'll bite into a soft, warm, and chocolaty treat in less than ten minutes. It's a satisfying little luxury achievable at any time of the day.

97: Variety of Chocolate Dipped Strawberries

Dive into the delightful world of chocolate-covered strawberries, a simple yet elegant treat for any occasion. Whether it's a romantic date, family gathering, or self-indulgence, these deliciously dressed-up fruits, created with your microwave, offer a burst of joy with every bite.

Servings: 4

Prepping Time: 10 minutes

Cook Time: 2 minutes

Difficulty: Easy

Ingredients:

- 1 pound of fresh strawberries
- 6 ounces of semi-sweet chocolate
- 2 ounces of white chocolate
- 2 ounces of dark chocolate

Step-by-Step Preparation:

1. Wash strawberries and pat dry thoroughly.

2. Melt semi-sweet chocolate in the microwave in 30-second intervals, stirring between each until smooth.
3. Dip strawberries into the semi-sweet chocolate, placing them on a wax paper-lined tray.
4. Repeat steps 2-3 for white and dark chocolate, drizzling the dipped strawberries for added design.
5. Refrigerate for at least 30 minutes before serving.

Nutritional Facts: (Per serving)

- ❖ Calories: 300
- ❖ Protein: 3 grams
- ❖ Carbohydrates: 35 grams
- ❖ Fat: 16 grams
- ❖ Fiber: 5 grams
- ❖ Sugar: 27 grams

Bask in the bliss of chocolate-coated elegance with this variety of chocolate-dipped strawberries. Easy to prepare yet beautifully sophisticated, they bring a touch of luxury to any table. Enjoy them as a sweet ending to a meal or as a thoughtful gift because nothing says 'I care' quite like hand-dipped strawberries.

98: Peanut Butter Chocolate Cake

Indulge in the richness of peanut butter and chocolate cake in your microwave. This luscious and flavorful recipe is perfect for satisfying your sweet tooth without much effort.

Servings: 2

Prepping Time: 10 Minutes

Cook Time: 3 Minutes

Difficulty: Easy

Ingredients:

- 4 tablespoons all-purpose flour
- 2 tablespoons unsweetened cocoa powder
- 4 tablespoons granulated sugar
- 1/8 teaspoon baking powder
- 3 tablespoons milk
- 2 tablespoons vegetable oil
- 2 tablespoons peanut butter
- 1/4 teaspoon vanilla extract
- A pinch of salt

Step-by-Step Preparation:

1. Mix flour, cocoa powder, sugar, and baking powder in a bowl.
2. Add milk, vegetable oil, peanut butter, vanilla extract, and a pinch of salt. Mix until well combined.
3. Pour the batter into a microwave-safe mug or ramekin.
4. Cook in the microwave for 3 minutes or until the cake is set.
5. Allow to cool for a few minutes before eating.

Nutritional Facts: (Per serving)

- Calories: 450
- Protein: 8g
- Carbohydrates: 54g
- Fat: 24g
- Fiber: 3g
- Sugar: 30g

A piece of heaven in a mug, this peanut butter chocolate cake is a quick, easy, and delightful treat. It's a perfect dessert for unexpected guests, a midnight snack, or chocolate-peanut butter comfort. Enjoy this delicious cake straight from your microwave to your mouth.

99: Pound Cake or Angel Food Cake

Experience the joy of baking without the oven with this simple yet delightful Microwave Pound Cake or Angel Food Cake—a perfect treat for last-minute guests or a quick dessert craving. I am offering a tender crumb that melts in your mouth with each bite.

Servings: 6

Prepping Time: 10 minutes

Cook Time: 10 minutes

Difficulty: Easy

Ingredients:

- 1 1/2 cups all-purpose flour
- 1 1/2 teaspoons baking powder
- 1/4 teaspoon salt
- 3/4 cup white sugar
- 1/2 cup unsalted butter, melted
- 1/2 cup milk
- 2 large eggs
- 1 teaspoon vanilla extract

Step-by-Step Preparation:

1. Combine all dry ingredients in a bowl.
2. Stir in the melted butter, milk, eggs, and vanilla extract until smooth.
3. Pour the mixture into a microwave-safe dish.
4. Microwave on high for 10 minutes or until a toothpick comes out clean when inserted into the center.
5. Allow to cool before serving.

Nutritional Facts: (Per serving)

- Calories: 320
- Fat: 14g
- Carbohydrates: 43g
- Protein: 6g
- Sodium: 200mg
- Sugar: 22g

Indulge in this heavenly, moist pound cake that is quick, easy, and incredibly satisfying. Whether you need a last-minute dessert or something sweet to accompany your afternoon tea, this recipe will surely be your microwave's best friend—no need for fancy tools or ingredients; just a simple, delicious cake in minutes.

100: Strawberry Cobbler Made From Ripe

Discover the joy of a quick and easy dessert with our Microwave Strawberry Cobbler recipe. This classic Southern delight transforms into a hassle-free sweet treat, perfect for any occasion.

Servings: 4

Prepping Time: 10 minutes

Cook Time: 5 minutes

Difficulty: Easy

Ingredients:

- 2 cups ripe fresh strawberries, hulled and halved
- 1/2 cup granulated sugar
- 1 cup all-purpose flour
- 1 teaspoon baking powder
- 1/2 cup milk
- 1/4 cup unsalted butter, melted

Step-by-Step Preparation:

1. Combine strawberries and 1/4 cup sugar in a bowl; set aside.

2. Mix flour, remaining sugar, and baking powder in another bowl.
3. Stir in milk and melted butter until combined.
4. Pour the mixture into a microwave-safe dish.
5. Top with strawberries.
6. Microwave on high for 5 minutes or until the topping is set.

Nutritional Facts: (Per serving)

- Calories: 310
- Carbs: 53g
- Protein: 4g
- Fat: 10g
- Fiber: 2g
- Sugar: 30g

Summertime will feel closer with every spoonful of this Microwave Strawberry Cobbler. Quick to prepare, this delightful dessert allows you to savor the sweet freshness of strawberries without spending hours in the kitchen. Perfect for both unexpected guests and planned gatherings. Enjoy!

Conclusion

As you come to the close of **"A Quick and Tasty Cookbook with 100 Easy Microwave Recipes"** we hope you have discovered the immense versatility and convenience that microwave cooking offers. Olivia Anderson's recipes have been designed to show you that it's possible to create delicious, nourishing, and exciting meals, all while saving time and reducing kitchen clutter.

This book was not only about providing quick and easy recipes but also about shifting perceptions and breaking away from the stereotype that microwave cooking is only for reheating leftovers or preparing pre-packaged meals. We hope you have discovered that the microwave can be your trusted partner in the kitchen, offering efficiency without compromising on taste.

Remember, these recipes are more than a list of ingredients and steps; they're a starting point. Feel free to experiment with flavors, swap ingredients, and make these dishes your own. That's the beauty of cooking, and it remains true, even with the simplicity and speed of the microwave.

As you continue your culinary journey, may each quick beep of your microwave remind you of the delicious possibilities that await within its walls. **"A Quick and Tasty Cookbook with 100 Easy Microwave Recipes"** is more than a book; it's a gateway to a new culinary world where speed, convenience, and flavor coexist harmoniously. Thank you for letting Olivia Anderson be part of your cooking adventures. Here's to many quick, tasty, and fulfilling meals ahead!

Printed in Great Britain
by Amazon